CASE STUDIES IN
CULTURAL ANTHROPOLOGY

GENERAL EDITORS
George and Louise Spindler
STANFORD UNIVERSITY

THE PORTLAND LONGSHOREMEN

PACIFIC NORTHWEST

〰〰〰 Rivers

- - - - - - - - Political Boundaries

THE PORTLAND LONGSHOREMEN

A Dispersed Urban Community

By

WILLIAM W. PILCHER

The State University College at Brockport, New York

HOLT, RINEHART AND WINSTON

NEW YORK   CHICAGO   SAN FRANCISCO   ATLANTA
DALLAS   MONTREAL   TORONTO   LONDON   SYDNEY

To Harry Pilcher

Cover photograph by Gordon Clark

Copyright © 1972 by Holt, Rinehart and Winston, Inc.
Library of Congress Catalog Card Number: 72-84398
ISBN: 0–03–091289–X
Printed in the United States of America
4 5 6 7   059   9 8 7 6 5 4 3 2

Foreword

About the Series

These case studies in cultural anthropology are designed to bring to students, in beginning and intermediate courses in the social sciences, insights into the richness and complexity of human life as it is lived in different ways and in different places. They are written by men and women who have lived in the societies they write about and who are professionally trained as observers and interpreters of human behavior. The authors are also teachers, and in writing their books they have kept the students who will read them foremost in their minds. It is our belief that when an understanding of ways of life very different from one's own is gained, abstractions and generalizations about social structure, cultural values, subsistence techniques, and the other universal categories of human social behavior become meaningful.

About the Author

William Pilcher was born in Everett, Washington, in 1930. His father was a longshoreman, as were several other of his close kinsmen. After dropping out of high school in the second year, he worked at many roughneck jobs in the Pacific Northwest, and after serving in the Marine Corps in Korea, became a member of the Portland local of the International Longshoremen's and Warehousemen's Union. After almost ten years as a full-time longshoreman, he began to work toward a B.A. in Social Science at Portland State College, financing his studies by working the night shift on the waterfront. He received his bachelor's degree in 1963. He then began work on his doctorate in anthropology at the University of Illinois, first specializing in linguistics and later shifting to urban anthropology and the study of the roughneck workers among whom he had been raised and spent most of his life. He received his Ph.D. in anthropology from the University of Illinois in 1970, taught at Western Michigan University, California State College, Long Beach, and is presently at The State University College at Brockport, New York.

About the Book

This case study of the Portland longshoremen is representative of a powerful new development in anthropology. Long dedicated to the study of technologically primitive societies or folk cultures and to traveling far afield for their study, many anthropologists are beginning now to turn to a study of communities and groups within contemporary American society. This attention is not focused solely upon ethnically differentiated groups. We are beginning to understand that all sectors of our society need anthropological study. Although many aspects of American society have been studied by sociologists, historians, and political scientists, relatively few have been approached with the field strategy and conceptual orientation of the anthropologist. The approach of the anthropologist is characterized by at least three major features: (1) heavy reliance upon participant-observation as a source of basic field data; (2) a transcultural perspective; and (3) contextualization within a broader frame of reference of the particular features under study.

William Pilcher has made very explicit his position as a participant-observer. He was a longshoreman himself for almost ten years, and his family, since his father was a longshoreman, is firmly a part of the longshoreman culture and social system. As he makes clear, it would have been impossible for him to gather the data necessary for this case study without his standing in this community. The transcultural perspective is less explicit. The longshoremen community is not compared directly to any other human community, though it is by implication. However, the conceptual organization of his case study in its attention to such matters as work culture, joking behavior, images, values, occupational genealogies, makes it clear that he has in his mind a model of cultural system derived from the transcultural experience of anthropology as a discipline. The third feature of an anthropological approach, the contextualization of what is being studied in a broader frame of reference, is manifested in this case study. The longshoremen community is placed in historical perspective by careful attention to the history and development of the Union and particularly the 1934 strike as a character-defining event. The longshoremen are also placed in the context of the broader community of Portland. His concern with a broad holistic approach is also indicated by his attention to such matters as the family and extra-work activities. These observations might be considered tangential or irrelevant if one were concerned only with the internal structure of the Longshoremen's Union or the longshoremen as a working group. These considerations are neither tangential nor irrelevant if we take a broader and characteristically anthropological view of the nature of human life.

There are, of course, shortcomings in this approach as it is developed in this case study. There is a relative lack of systematic statistical information on income, possessions, work periods, family size, household expenditures, etc. There is also a lack of systematic attitudinal data. The latter would have been, given the particular circumstances of study, probably almost impossible to obtain. The former might be obtainable with a very substantial investment of time requiring considerable resources beyond that of the single investigator. Like most anthropologists, William Pilcher has put his faith in his knowledge of the working of the system and its ancillary parts from the inside. As studies of contemporary American and other urban or urbanizing communities develop further, doubtless the models of research and the techniques with which they are carried out will produce satisfaction for both those who believe only in "hard data" and those who believe only in the "soft data" gathered by the participant-observer.

Stanford, California   GEORGE AND LOUISE SPINDLER
                                         General Editors

Preface

Unlike many other categories of workers, the Portland longshoremen form a distinct internal community in the Portland metropolitan area. The primary purpose of this case study is to describe this community, but a mere description would beg the question of how this phenomenon came about. Much of the description, therefore, will deal with the processes which forged a cohesive community out of a mere aggregate of roughneck workers. The most important preconditions for the formation of the group and its central organizing institution, the union, are the geographical and cultural backgrounds of the longshoremen which gave the group its culturally homogeneous nature as well as its predisposition toward left-wing unionism. The 1934 longshore strike really marks the founding of the Portland Longshore Union, and, as I will explain at length, gives the group its social charter, much in the way that a revolutionary war has functioned for larger sociopolitical entities. Indeed it is almost a mistake to class the Portland Longshore Union together with other unions, for its functions are not simply those of a collective bargaining agent. It has many of the aspects of a voluntary mutual assistance association and a social club. It provides the political structure of the group, legitimizes status within the group, and allows men of ability and ambition the opportunity to gain status in the eyes of their fellows.

The cultural background of the group members is important in many ways other than in giving the union its unique left-wing stance. The predominantly old-line Americans and Scandinavians agree wholeheartedly on the principle of social egalitarianism, and thus reject the concept of social mobility as intrinsically worthless. To these people, any attempt to display superior social status is repugnant. On the other hand, attempt to improve one's financial lot through striving for education or other means is seen as worthwhile and praiseworthy, as are efforts to gain educational skills useful to the union or the work. Prestige is readily granted to individuals who have distinguished themselves in approved areas of activities such as serving in union office, simply being good longshoremen, or in the sports activities of the group. The roots of this group lie deep in midwestern rural America, and they do not share the modern middle-class abhorrence of physical violence. Thus men who are noted fist fighters also have a certain prestige within the group so long as they adhere to the group norms of fair play and are not bullies.

Again, because many of the values and attitutdes of the longshore group, as well as many features of the occupation are those of an older America, it is the men who are central. Most of the men's activities are directed toward the welfare and happiness of their families, and nearly all the longshoremen are family men, but the men are central to the economy and welfare of the group and thus are central to this study.

Moreover, my only available source of information concerning the roles of women was my own personal experience growing up in a longshore family and visiting in the homes of others. For this reason I have not expanded on the activities of the women although I am sure there is ample material for another study to be carried out by a woman. She would not face the risk of being considered an intruder into the homes of the younger longshoremen. Access to free communication with the women was restricted by the inevitable suspicion of my intent, which I was never foolish enough to arouse by attempting to interview a woman when her husband was not present, and when he was present, the wife would always grant him the center of the stage and defer to his opinions.

Again, as in most groups, it is the activities of the males as the public agents of the group that are most distinctive, whatever may lie behind their public actions. The situation is analogous to that of the Iroquois, where the men were always the political leaders and agents of their clans, although their positions reflected the will of their clanswomen.

I wish here to offer my thanks to all the longshoremen, both old-timers and Johnny-come-latelies like myself for the assistance they gave me in carrying out this study. My thanks are also offered for the financial support given me by the University of Illinois and to the faculty of the Department of Anthropology, especially Julian Steward, Oscar Lewis, and Demitri Shimkin for their help and for their patience in dealing with what must have been one of the most difficult graduate students in their experience. I also would like to express my gratitude to Charles Frantz and Duane Metzger for pushing me toward the cultural study of longshoremen, and to Alberta Brose who typed and edited the manuscript.

Brockport, New York   WILLIAM W. PILCHER
1972

Contents

1 / Introduction

The community has long been the basic unit of analysis in anthropology. The ideal unit has been what Redfield termed "the little community," small, isolated, and clearly marked off from other communities (Redfield 1955). Such a community is, of course, much easier to study in both conceptual and practical terms than one that is large, vaguely demarcated, and embedded among or in close proximity to others. Moreover, this approach has allowed the analyst to treat the community as though it were a laboratory specimen artificially separated from contact with contaminating outside influences, and thus to study its morphology and internal processes without regard for other variables. The distortions introduced by this approach, since no community ever exists in total isolation from all others, would be many times magnified in the case of internal urban communities where the criteria of relative isolation, small size, and clearly defined boundaries are almost impossible to meet. The city itself poses an even more difficult problem due to its complex internal morphology, and in cognizance of this, social scientists have tended to narrow their focus to limited aspects of relatively small internal urban groups rather than to attempt to analyze the urban aggregate. This has, however, led us into yet another problem: we have many studies of limited aspects, such as consumption patterns, of urban segments defined by many varying sets of criteria, but very few that can properly be called community studies.

This is in large part due to the difficulty of defining an internal urban community, which is at least partially attributable to the vague manner in which the term "community" has been used in the social sciences. Despite its great longevity, this term has remained ill-defined and is used in many different ways. Thus we find this same term applied to such very different phenomena as Chan Kom, New York City, and Cornerville (Whyte 1943). Generally, those phenomena classified as communities have been some sort of territorially defined aggregate. There are, however, two basic components to the concept of community as it is used in anthropology: first, there is a social component, the implication of a social structure and a social group; and, second, there is a territorial component, the implication of the contiguous residence of community members. These two components are in no sense contradictory but rather complementary, for the social and territorial units are usually coextensive. However, one often receives the impression that the territorial aspect is more important than the social aspect in defining the commu-

1

nity. This proposition is of course ludicrous, for if there is no social group, no internal structure, there is no community.

The forces that have led urban anthropology to dwell so heavily on the territorial unit in the urban context are not difficult to discover. Urban anthropology received its greatest impetus with the vast influx of rural people into urban centers following World War II. Anthropologists entered the urban context following the same peoples they had previously studied in their rural homes where the territorial and social components of the native communities were always coextensive. Moreover, these rural migrants, usually poor and lacking the skills and contacts necessary to rapid upward mobility in the urban centers, tended (and still tend) to cluster in those residential areas most compatible with their meager financial resources, thus forming territorial aggregates. It is just these aggregates that modern urban anthropology has focused on. This has resulted primarily in the study of recent migrants to the city, of slums and ethnic neighborhoods territorially defined, which do not always constitute meaningful social units or communities.

While new migrants to the cities have been the subject of intense anthropological activity, the established residents of cities have been all but ignored. Even sociology has given scant attention to such long-term residents, which presents something of a paradox, for while urban anthropology and sociology have been much concerned with the adaptation and adjustment of rural migrants to the cities, they have tended to ignore the groups of older residents to which the migrants must eventually adjust if they are to make a successful adaptation to urban life. In other words, an important part of the urban context has not been subject to scientific scrutiny. Moreover, these segments of urban societies must be carefully studied if we are ever to produce anything but a fragmented and faulty picture of the internal social and cultural morphology of cities. There is, of course, no reason to believe that these modern, urbanized people are residentially clustered on any basis whatsoever other than rough measure of income, and income has proved to be a notoriously bad indicator of social ties or even class (Gordon 1958).

Other criteria for establishing a basic unit of analysis may be preferable to residence or ethnic affiliation in the urban context, for residence has never been more than a convenient starting place for social analysis. There are many other possible bases around which meaningful social groups (communities) may be formed. Among these are religion, voluntary associations, special interests, and occupation (Steward 1956). Within modern urban centers occupation presents itself as the most likely starting place for a number of reasons: first, all but the very wealthy must somehow earn a living; second, as Everett Hughes has noted (1958), a man's work is the one most significant fact in his life; and third, primary social identity in industrial societies tends to be based on occupation. Indeed, the lack of an occupational identity may be seen as a social pathology, for few urban people lack such an identity save those who share what Lewis has termed the "culture of poverty" (Lewis 1966). Many occupational studies, especially of blue-collar workers, have been made by sociologists, but here too the accent has been on recent migrants, slum communities, and ephemeral ethnic association (Miller and Riessman 1964). Only a very few have focused on occupational groups, and only Lipset *et al.* (1962) have dealt with any of the aspects of the community. This study is in many ways designed to correct this situation by making as complete a description of an occupationally based community and the institutions which give it its coherency and continuity as space will allow.

THE LONGSHOREMEN

The community on which this study is centered consists of the approximately twelve hundred longshoremen who work in and around Portland, Oregon, together with their families. All longshoremen in the Port of Portland are either members of Local 8 of the International Longshoremen's and Warehousemen's Union or are carried on the union permit rolls. The International Longhoremen's and Warehousemen's Union (hereafter ILWU) represents nearly all of the longshoremen of the West Coast of the United States, including Alaska and the Hawaiian Islands, and Canada. The ILWU not only represents the Hawaiian longshoremen and warehouse workers, but also nearly all unionized workers in the Hawaiian Islands. Although they are often confused, the ILWU is in no way affiliated with the International Longshoremen's Association (hereafter ILA) which represents the vast majority of East and Gulf Coast longshoremen and many of the longshoremen of the Great Lakes and the Eastern Canadian Ports. Prior to 1937 the West Coast Longshoremen had comprised the Pacific Coast branch of the ILA, when the rebellion of the West Coast longshoremen under the leadership of Harry Bridges resulted in the formation of the ILWU as an independent union. Since that time the two longshore unions have not only been unaffiliated but, for the most part, bitterly at odds.

There are three levels of organization within the ILWU. The overall administrative level is the international union. Just below the international level are the area organizations, each encompassing a number of local unions and a fairly large geographical area. The lowest level is the local union. Each port or port complex (such as the Los Angeles complex) has its own semiautonomous local union. Each local is composed of the longshoremen who work in the port and the officials elected from their ranks. Again, each port has three ILWU locals, although only one of these is a longshore local. Other than the longshore local there is a local representing the ships' clerks and another which represents the walking bosses or general foremen. The ships' clerks have traditionally been recruited from outside of the longshore group and have always been represented by a separate local, but the walking bosses are all recruited from the ranks of the longshore local and only have a separate collective bargaining representative because it is required by law. For this reason and because the ships' clerks are essentially white-collar workers, they are not included in this study, but the walking bosses are treated as part of the longshore group. The walking bosses' local is not dealt with separately because of its very brief history and insignificant size.

QUESTIONS TO BE ANSWERED

Are the Portland longshoremen and their families a meaningful social group? Or are they only an aggregate of persons working at the same job? An occupational community exists when the individuals working in a specific occupation share certain complexes of skills, have a community of interest, strongly identify as a group, and tend to associate only with people who work at the same occupation or for some other reason are felt to be members of the ingroup (Lipset, Trow, and Coleman 1962). This definition is weak only in that it does not explicitly recognize the work and associated factors such as the strong involvement of a labor union in the day-to-day life of the workers and their families as integrating community institutions, a viewpoint that will be taken throughout this work.

Does the group bear a distinctive subculture vis-à-vis other groups of workers? The greater part of the culture of the longshoremen is certainly shared with all other Americans. Their clothing, household furnishings and appliances, vehicles, and nearly every other material item they use originate in highly standardized commercial manufacture. Moreover, their children attend public schools, and they are subject at all times to the impact of mass media and advertising. Nevertheless, as members of a strongly cohesive, distinctive occupational group with its own values and sanctions, they are not entirely subject to the conformity-producing forces operating throughout the entire society.

Other questions must be asked if this presentation is to be a dynamic rather than a static description of the Portland longshoremen. What are the historical processes that formed the group and the subculture? This can only be answered by historical research, by examining documents and interviewing people who took part in historically relevant events. The year 1922 has been chosen as a baseline because it is a year of immense importance to the formation of the present longshore group.

The final major question is how this community and its way of life have been maintained despite the impact of local and national level institutions and the rapid social and industrial change of recent times. What are the features of the local and national context that operate in the city of Portland and to what extent do they actually affect the Portland longshoremen?

HOW THE QUESTIONS ARE ANSWERED

Before I began graduate work in anthropology at the University of Illinois, I had been a full-time longshoreman and a member of the Portland Local of the ILWU for more than twelve years, and had spent the majority of my life in the company of longshoremen and their families in Oregon and Washington. Two of my brothers are at present working on the waterfront and are members of the ILWU, one in Seattle, Washington, and the other in Portland, Oregon. Another of my brothers has been a merchant seaman for many years. My father is a charter member of the ILWU and was very active in union affairs until his retirement in 1957. Not only was my father an active union member, he was instrumental in the organization of the northern Washington ports and was at one time loaned out to help organize a strike of the timber workers. I owe much of my data concerning the early organization of the Portland Longshore Union and early conditions on the waterfront to him and to other old-time longshoremen who assisted me out of friendship for him. My father and his old-timer friends were not simply men who happened to be working on the waterfront, but men who were very important in shaping the events of the time. This is perhaps best illustrated by pointing out that one of these old-timers was Harry Bridges, the President of the International Longshoremen's and Warehousemen's Union. It is, however, inevitable that each of these men should give a somewhat different account of each event and that each should place his own interpretation upon it; therefore, the accounts given of recent waterfront history and events are the result of much crosschecking and collating of information received from many different people who participated in those events.

I began this research with a large fund of knowledge gained through many years of personal experience on the waterfront. This knowledge, however, was not sufficient to allow me to prepare a descriptive and analytical treatise without extensive research into the history and present condition of the Portland longshore group, the Union, the city, and the state. In some ways my previous knowledge hindered me because I believed, when I began my research, that I knew the answers to many questions and was surprised when my own data proved me wrong. For example, I believed, as do many people who are familiar with the waterfront, that the ideological orientation of the union was derived from communist and socialist sources. I found that although these organizations had some influence in the founding of the Union, the ideological orientation has been derived almost directly from that of the Industrial Workers of the World and midwestern Populism.

During the entire eighteen months of research, I was a member of ILWU, Local 8, and worked part-time as a longshoreman. This had not been my original intent, but I found certain kinds of data impossible to obtain in any other way; moreover this validated my role as a member of the longshore group and demonstrated that I did not consider myself in any way superior to the other longshoremen because of my education, a point upon which I was immediately challenged when I began my research. This approach would have been extremely difficult, if not impossible, had I not already been a member of the Longshore Union and a skilled longshoreman, and hence a member of the group.

I had originally intended to use a structured interview technique based on a detailed questionnaire to gather data on a number of variables such as religion, union activity, employment histories, voluntary association membership, political affiliations and beliefs, marital status and history, education, and occupational genealogies. This met with very limited success. Only when I was interviewing veteran longshoremen, who had been involved in historical events concerning the establishment of the union and who consequently felt a deep sense of having taken part in events of real historical significance, was I able to use the questionnaire. Even in these cases, I was usually unable to hold the informant to the format. My most valuable tool at these times was my tape recorder, since I could guide the

Ethnographer interviewing a former Wobbly concerning details of the 1922 strike. (Photo by Gordon Clark)

narration back to points that had been passed by and later order the data from a transcription of the tapes. In this manner, I compiled some twenty direct case histories and occupational genealogies, much information concerning over 180 other persons, the basic pattern of affinal ("in-law") and consanguineal ("blood") relationships within the group, and nearly all of the recent history of the union. This last item was of extreme importance, because there is very little literature on the subject and most of it is undependable. The literature published by the various waterfront employers' associations was extremely slanted and systematically in error.

In 1934, the employers attributed the longshore strike to the influence of the Communist party, although the core of active union men was composed of former Wobblies (Industrial Workers of the World). The union literature is little better and most of it is concerned with affairs in San Francisco. Indeed, one would receive the impression that there was almost no activity in any port except San Francisco, if the union literature were to be taken at face value.

With only a few exceptions, attempts to use any type of formal interview to gather information from the younger longshoremen met with almost instant rejection. The personal questions concerning union affiliation and occupational histories were easily accepted, but queries even tangentially approaching the subject of the informant's family were invariably seen as attempts to pry into affairs that were none of my business. These queries were almost universally rejected and further attempts to gather the data merely served to irritate and alienate the informant. I found that I could in no way persuade these men to cooperate. I could only ask for cooperation and had nothing with which to reciprocate, since unlike many informants, the longshoremen were not in need of any form of assistance that I could offer them and what prestige I possessed accrued not from my status as an anthropologist or scholar but rather from my status as a member of the longshore group.

To circumvent this obstacle, I relied more and more on the traditional anthropological role of the participant-observer, and drew heavily upon my status as a union member. I had already taken up my union membership and attended union meetings, but now I went back to work on the docks and ships. Although this approach is ideally less efficient than an interview technique, in practice it was much more effective. Questions that would not have been answered in the formal context of an interview were freely answered in on-the-job "bull sessions," or in the informal atmosphere of a restaurant or tavern. Genealogical information and family data were obtained by volunteering some bit of information about my own family or genealogy, such as "Did you know my grandfather was a frontier marshal?" This ploy was almost certain to elicit information about the fathers and other ancestors of most of the men within range of my voice. The data were available just so long as it did not appear that I was making any real effort to obtain them. In this manner I obtained genealogical and other material on over two hundred men.

There is no intent here to give the impression that the Portland longshoremen did not try to assist me or that they tried to prevent my research, because the majority of the men I talked to tried to help me in any way they could; however, many of them did not fully understand my purposes, and it is one feature of the long-shore subculture that one does not inquire too deeply into another individual's family affairs. Portland longshoremen, like most Americans, feel strongly that certain subjects, such as family affairs and one's sex life, are not legitimate subjects of inquiry, even for close friends. Information on these subjects was often volunteered, but attempts to probe beyond the volunteered statements were regarded as simple violations of good manners and taste. I feel that the longshoremen are perhaps more strict in these respects than most Americans, and this is one of their distinguishing subcultural characteristics. It is exactly in this sort of emphasis or lack of emphasis that this or any other modern subcultural segment is distinctive from all others. Few of the values of the group are unique: they are shared by nearly all other Americans and in some cases by nearly all peoples of European ancestry. However, the particular conformation of emphasis or lack of emphasis is probably unique to the longshoremen and certain other similar groups of workers.

THE SETTING

The site of this study is Portland, Oregon, the second largest port on the Pacific coast in total waterborne commerce. Located at the confluence of the Willamette and Columbia Rivers where the northward flowing Willamette empties into the Columbia almost exactly 100 miles from the Pacific Ocean, Portland owes much of its prominence as a seaport to this location. The Willamette south of Portland will not support seagoing vessels, but it is and has long been a major route for barge traffic carrying cargo to and from Portland, and once was a principal carrier of log rafts destined for the docks and sawmills of the city. The Columbia contributes even more to the volume of shipping that passes through Portland. The Cascade Mountains exceed 12,000 feet at the higher peaks, and many of the passes are narrow and tortuous, making the broad gorge of the Columbia by far the easiest shipping route between the Columbia Plateau wheatlands to the east and the sea. The Columbia Gorge cuts through the Cascade Mountains at almost grade level and thus provides a thoroughfare for barges and an easy route for rail, highway, and air traffic.

Other than tourism there are only two significant industries in Oregon. East of the Cascades the state is devoted to agriculture, as is much of southern Oregon and most of the Willamette Valley. In the Cascade Mountains and to the west of the mountains, the major industry is timber. Portland began its history as a seaport with the lumber schooner trade plying the Pacific coast between the more heavily populated areas of southern California and San Francisco. Much of the early lumber trade was also with the East Coast of the United States and the Orient. The East Coast trade expanded over the years as did the trade with Europe until these areas, along with the Orient, became the major markets for Oregon lumber. This has also been very much the history of other ports in the Northwest with the exception of Seattle–Tacoma, which early became much more closely associated with the Alaska trade. Today the Northwest supplies most of the construction timber and lumber for the United States, Europe, and Japan, the China trade having terminated with the downfall of the Nationalist regime of Chiang Kai-shek. The heaviest shipments of cargo leaving Portland today consist of bulk wheat brought in from the inland wheat growing areas, and the lumber trade through Portland has much declined with the steady recession of timber suitable for cutting from the Portland area. The many sawmills that once operated in Portland itself are now closed with two small exceptions, but Portland's history is closely bound to the history of the timber industry in the Northwest, a fact that will be expanded in the section on the history of the area.

The total population of Oregon is just under two million, of which nearly a third live in or near the Portland metropolitan area. The official population of the city proper was 365,000 in 1966 and 774,205 for the surrounding five-county area. Large parts of the eastern and southern parts of the state are very thinly settled, and Portland is by far the largest city in terms of population. No other city in Oregon exceeds a total of 100,000 residents. The ethnic composition of the state is primarily North European, and immigration into Oregon has always been predominantly native American. The first immigrants came from New England and the Old South, but by far the greatest numbers originated in the Midwest. The largest groups of foreign-born migrants were from the British Isles, Canada, Germany, and Scandinavia. None of these ethnic groups, however, was at any time of great political or cultural significance to the state. At no time did the foreign-born population of Oregon exceed one-sixth of the total population, and this figure was only reached during the decades of most intensive immigration around the turn of the century (Pollard 1951). The formation of ethnic minority groups is greatly retarded if they do not bring community level institutions with them and if their numbers are not great enough to support such institutions. The foreign-born immigrants arrived in Oregon as individuals or as small family groups and had to face the task of adjusting to the native Oregonians without the support of large numbers of their fellow countrymen. Only the Germans and Scandinavians ever displayed any of the symptoms of becoming nationally conscious ethnic groups. They did form national societies, but these societies were only local branches of large national associations with their headquarters in the East or Midwest, such as the Sons of Norway. Some of these societies still exist, but in their relatively short existence they have developed primarily into social clubs that sponsor affairs such as dances and have lost almost all other significance.

Cultural similarity or lack of similarity is also an important element in the assimilation of ethnic minorities. The British lost all ethnic identity within the first generation, probably because of their near cultural identity with the native Americans. The Germans and Scandinavians took longer to lose their ethnic identities, but were nearly all completely assimilated by the second generation, and have formed no ethnic neighborhoods or other enclaves such as characterize Chicago and New York. These national groups are all much closer in their national cultures to the native Americans than are the southern and eastern Europeans that populated most of the large eastern urban centers, and since they were predominantly Protestant, they are not even as distinct as the Irish in New York and Chicago. They did not have so much as an exclusive church to orient themselves around, since the churches to which they belonged had already been established in this country and had large congregations of native Americans into which the immigrants were readily absorbed.

There is very little difference between the ethnic composition and history of the state as a whole and that of the city of Portland. There were small ethnic neighborhoods in Portland at one time, but these lasted for little more than one generation and were never of any size or influence in the city. The last of these was a little Jewish neighborhood in Southwest Portland that was destroyed by urban renewal in 1960. A predominantly Negro neighborhood exists, but it too is small and of little influence. The majority of its residents are recent migrants to Portland and do not figure in the history of the Portland longshoremen until very recently.

NATURE OF THE INDUSTRY

The longshore industry can only be described as very irregular—if not erratic. Ships must be serviced when they arrive in port if their economic potential is to be realized. A ship sitting at anchor in a harbor suffers from depreciation of its original value as much as it does when it is at sea, but when it is at sea with cargo in its holds, it is earning money for its owners. It is not earning profits when it is sitting idle or being loaded, and thus the owners of cargo ships are always impatient to have their ships serviced and at sea. Shipping schedules are only loosely adhered to for a number of reasons. Weather is alway a prime factor. Storms at sea, and most especially storms off the mouth of the Columbia, where crossing the bar is a difficult task in anything but the best weather, may throw ships off their announced schedules for several days. Many ships also pick up cargo where and when they can and their schedules again have to be tentative. Engine and gear breakdowns and difficulty in loading or discharging in some ports make for more irregularity. The net result is that on some days the harbor is crowded with ships, some of which cannot be worked with the regular work force, and on other days the harbor may be empty or have only one or two ships at its docks. For the longshoreman this means that he may work for several weeks at seven days per week with many overtime hours to his credit, followed by a considerable layoff or a period when a week's earnings consist of only one or two days' pay. The longshore industry is one of the first to be affected by shifts in the world market, but this does not change the pattern of the work; it only shortens or lengthens the "boom or bust" periods. Ships still pile up in the port when international trade is low and there are idle periods when trade is high.

Since longshoremen, like other people, must have some minimum income and also present to themselves and the world an acceptable self-image, they have developed several adaptive reactions to this situation. The first of these I have designated the "feast-or-famine" philosophy. This involves treating the most undesirable aspect of longshore life, the unpredictability of the work, as a desirable mode of existence. The erratic nature of the work is translated into freedom from a rigid work regime with an emphasis on the economic gains to be made during boom periods. Such an unpredictable income would seem to be a fact of life that would make for a good deal of personal anxiety on the part of the longshoreman and his family. One of the ways in which this anxiety is alleviated by the longshoreman is the presentation of a devil-may-care image to the world. They present themselves as nonchalant roughnecks, unconcerned with the irregularity of their work, and well able to handle any problems that may arise. However, this equanimity is much bolstered by two other aspects of the longshoreman's adaptation to his economic environment: the development of secondary sources of income that can be activated when the waterfront is at low ebb; and union control of the hiring system and a system of rotating hiring that have the twin effects of distributing the work evenly among all of the longshoremen during lean periods and avoiding the sort of corrupt hiring practices that are typical of many of the world's waterfronts.

2 / The community

The cultural basis of the Portland longshore community has its roots in two primary sources. First, and perhaps foremost, it arises out of the very similar cultural backgrounds of the vast majority of its members, its old-line American character; and second, it is very much a function of the nature of the work, for there has obviously been much selection for certain personality types among the men.

Although longshoremen are little known to most Americans, except perhaps through such badly distorted representations as the movie *On the Waterfront* or New York Crime Commission reports on the New York waterfront, they are very visible and well known to many residents of port cities. Everywhere, they have a colorful reputation, much of which is undeserved. Partially, this reputation as crude, brawling, heavy-drinking, thieving ne'er-do-wells is derived, as was noted by Barnes (1915) in New York, from the waterfront drifters who hang around the waterfront picking up a few days work during peak periods; but it is also in large part due to the carefully cultivated virile image projected by the regular longshoremen. They like to see themselves as rough and ready individuals, and that is the image that they project both to outsiders and to one another. It would be a mistake not to take this image seriously, for no image of self can be maintained unless one is willing and at least marginally able to demonstrate when challenged that he has the attributes that he advertises. This image derives in part from the recent frontier nature of the area, but as will be explained in the pages following, it is also a very necessary adjunct of being involved in longshore work.

ETHNIC COMPOSITION AND DEMOGRAPHY

Among the Portland longshoremen the only noteworthy group of foreign immigrants other than English and Canadians, who tend rapidly to become indistinguishable from native-born Americans, are the Scandinavians, and although they differ slightly from the rest of the longshoremen, the pattern of their arrival on the waterfront and assimilation into the longshore group tends to be very similar to that of the other longshoremen. A workout of ethnic proportions as indicated by surnames reveals that the largest number of non–Anglo-Saxon names are Scandina-

TABLE 1   PROPORTIONS OF ETHNIC AFFILIATION OF PORTLAND LONGSHOREMEN

	Number	% of Total
Membership List 12/1/64		
Anglo–Saxon	600	57.14
Scandinavian	200	19.05
German	150	14.28
All Others	100	9.52
	1050	100.00
Living Pensioners 5/1/66		
Anglo–Saxon	206	51.50
Scandinavian	118	29.50
German	53	13.25
All Others	23	5.75
	400	100.00
Deceased Pensioners 5/1/66		
Anglo–Saxon	135	44.44
Scandinavian	102	32.62
German	32	17.92
All Others	10	5.02
	279	100.00

vian and the next largest, German, but this really has little significance. For example, I asked one of the longshoremen with a Scandinavian name and a Norwegian accent where he had been born in Norway, and he answered that he had been born in Fargo, North Dakota, and that his father had been born in Minnesota. Only about a third of the men with Scandinavian names were actual immigrants, and this was true of even fewer of those with German names. Intermarriage within the group accounts for much of this as does the simple fact of old-settler ancestry. A Scandinavian or German name often only indicates a male of that nationality somewhere in one's ancestry. (I am myself an old-line American with an English name, but my mother's surname was Welsh and her mother's was Dutch, while my paternal grandmother's maiden name was Irish.)

Men came to the waterfront for many reasons. Most came from farming backgrounds, but many were also loggers (lumberjacks), commercial fishermen, and sailors who wanted to settle down from their semitransient way of life. But the progression across the country, generation by generation, is very typical of the group: let us say from Pennsylvania to Kansas or Illinois, then to Idaho, and finally to Oregon. One old-timer's case will serve to illustrate this point.

My grandfather was born in Virginia and my father was born in Missouri. I was born in Montana in 1908. My dad sold out in Montana and bought a ranch in southern Idaho. Dad lived on that ranch for five years, and then he got tired of fighting the snow and he heard about southern Oregon. He thought he wanted to go to a place where he didn't have to feed in the wintertime. He was a stockman. So he bought a ranch in southern Oregon. When I was 14 years old and in the eighth grade, my dad died. And I took a job working a night shift, and I went to school in the daytime. I worked from four to midnight in a sawmill. I finished the eighth grade, and in the fall I started to work on the Southern Pacific section [laying track]. I got fired and replaced by a Mexican when they found out I was only 14 years old. When I was 15, I worked as a summer smoke chaser for the Forest Service. Me and my dog. I came out that fall and they kept me down there and I shingled the Ranger's house and everything, and I worked the whole winter sharpening tools. I went out and was smoke chaser again that summer. Well, that fall I quit because I wanted to go to sea. But instead of going to sea I run into some guys and they was buying caulk boots, and they were going to work in the woods. My first job was greasing skids. I worked in the woods until I was 16. I decided to get a little traveling, and in those days when a kid left home he went on the tramp—what we called on the tramp. And I left Cottage Grove in a boxcar and I come back a year later in a boxcar. I'd been all over the United States. Then we went back to Idaho. I worked in the hayfields. My mother worked for an old rancher. I pitched hay ten hours a day for three dollars a day. I finished with that and we went up and picked apples. And when mother and I got done that fall we had 1,700 dollars in the bank. And the bank went broke. That was that, so I come down to Portland. I worked in the woods a while. By that time they'd got choker setters down to four dollars a day. He charged a dollar and a half for board. I couldn't quite see driving fifteen miles on a Mulligan car out to the job— and high ball outfit—for four dollars a day and get out of it with two and a half. I saw a bunch of guys with hooks in their pockets and so I followed a bunch of them down one morning. I knew these guys was going to work. I kind of liked their looks. They were a rugged bunch of boys. More out of curiosity than anything else I followed them. And that's where the Horse Thief— we called him—hired me to work on this log job. That was in June of 1927.

These men stayed on the waterfront for a set of reasons best stated by the same old-timer quoted above.

I told my mother, this is a stop gap, I want to get enough money to buy a ranch. But it seemed as though—oh, we banked our money in the Hibernia Bank on Third and Washington, and we got quite a little bit together. I don't know, twelve or thirteen hundred dollars. And that bank went broke. And it seemed as though one thing after another happened all through the years. And then I will admit the waterfront began to get to me. And I would think to myself, now I've just barely got an eighth grade education. Now where can I work now where I can make forty-five dollars a week? Because in this crowd that I was running around with there were kids working in banks, a couple of tailors, this and that, and I had more money than any of them. And I got to thinking— everything was all adding up. There was the freedom. There was the quick pay. You didn't have to wait a month for your pay. When you went up the gang-plank, the mate would pay you off in gold. Every job was different. Every ship was different. Every man you worked with, you worked with a different man every day. You met all kinds, types, every kind of man in the world. You got to see the whole world passing right there in front of your eyes. I guess I fell in love with the waterfront.

RESIDENCE AND THE CITY

Although they are a tightly integrated social group, the Portland longshoremen are scattered throughout the city in a completely random fashion, and there is no clustering around the docks or the hiring hall. There are two main factors involved in this. The first factor is the nature of the city: there is very little fractionalization of the city. Neighborhood lines are not clearly drawn, and there are no ethnic neighborhoods since there are no large ethnic groups to support them. Low cost housing may be and often is intermingled with high cost housing in a manner that would be deeply disturbing to city planners, and there are no clearly demarcated "good" neighborhoods. The only real neighborhood in the city is the Negro ghetto centered around Williams Avenue and Russell Street. The hiring hall is located in an industrial area that would accommodate few longshoremen even if they would live there, and the areas close around most of the docks are also heavily industrial. The docks are stretched out along the Willamette River over a distance of some ten miles which would also make it impractical for the longshoremen to try to live close to their work, since they do not know from day to day at which dock they will be working.

The second factor determining residence is the affluence and attitudes of the longshoremen. Most of the Portland longshoremen can afford to live in almost any kind of housing available in the city. The earnings listed in Table 2 show an aver-

TABLE 2   LONGSHOREMEN'S AVERAGE EARNINGS, 1966

		Number of Men	Hours	Average Annual Earnings	Hours	Average Annual Earnings
Southern California	Reg. A	2,929	1,740	$8,838	33.5	$170
	Reg. B	772	1,371	6,385	26.4	123
San Francisco	Reg. A	2,918	1,919	9,850	36.9	189
	Reg. B	985	1,817	8,492	34.9	163
Oregon	Reg. A	2,050	1,777	8,992	34.1	173
	Reg. B	547	1,576	7,294	30.3	140
Washington	Reg. A	2,031	1,825	9,369	35.1	180
	Reg. B	411	1,451	7,124	27.9	137
Pacific Coast (includes Stockton and Eureka)	Reg. A	10,522	1,793	9,162	34.4	176
	Reg. B	2,544	1,733	8,156	33.3	157

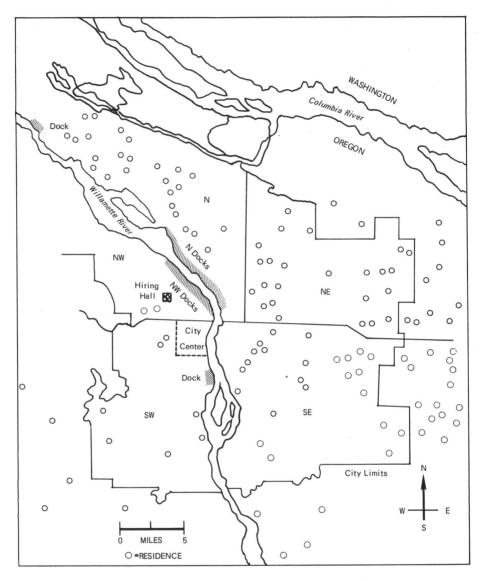

FIGURE 1   Residence pattern of longshoremen in Portland, Oregon

age of 8,992 dollars for the year 1966 for class A longshoremen in the State of Oregon. This figure is slightly misleading since the figures include ports such as Astoria and Newport which are frequently depressed. The figures for Portland should be somewhat nearer the figures given for San Francisco. Another problem is that no figures are available for income not earned on the waterfront, and in many cases this income is considerable because of the outside economic activities of the longshoremen. The value of fringe benefits such as the longshoremen's complete service coverage for medical care at the Bess Kaiser Hospital and complete dental care for children also tend to swell the longshoremen's real income. The figures are also depressed by the mingling of income figures from all age groups. Many of the middle-aged and older men do not attempt to work full-time: their homes are paid for, their children have left home, and they often have significant savings.

Combined with this affluence is the working-class propensity to choose a residence by the nature of the house rather than by the neighborhood. Longshoremen, like many other workers, will live in any house that is compatible with their income. Most of the men and their families live in medium sized well kept homes, but those in financial straits may occupy substandard housing while others have homes commensurate with upper middle-class incomes. Another factor that contributes to the scattered pattern of residence is the avidity with which many of the men pursue horticultural avocations. Such pursuits are better followed near the edge or outside of the city, therefore many of the Portland longshoremen live outside of Portland.

OCCUPATIONAL GENEALOGIES

The occupational genealogies of the Portland longshoremen display an interesting pattern, although part of the pattern was predictable because of the patterns of interrelationship among the members of the group. The most common occupation for a longshoreman's father is longshoring, followed in order by logging and farming. For grandfathers, the pattern is reversed, farming being the most common followed closely by logging and longshoring. The predominance of farmers in the second ascending generation is not particularly significant, because it merely reflects the character of the nation at a particular point in time. The likelihood that any given ascendant* will be a farmer is greater with each ascending generation, which is true of any occupational group in any modern nation.

The list of occupations of the ascendants of the Portland longshoremen is extensive: there are longshoremen, loggers, truckdrivers, construction workers, sailors, policemen, firemen, horsetraders, housepainters, gunsmiths, blacksmiths, and other self-employed skilled workers. There are also businessmen, professionals, engineers, teachers, clergymen, and politicians. The most significant thing about this list—and it is not exhaustive—is that it contains no clerical or managerial workers, and only one factory worker, an immigrant whose father was a European businessman. These occupations may be grouped into six major categories:

1. Roughneck workers such as longshoremen, sailors and loggers. Men who perform their tasks primarily out of doors, whose work schedules are very flexible, and whose competence is evaluated in terms of flexibility, of skills and physical fitness. A sort of Jack-of-all-trades.
2. Self-employed and other skilled workers.
3. Professionals, such as lawyers and medical doctors.
4. Semiprofessionals such as teachers and engineers.
5. Government workers and politicians.
6. Businessmen.

* Parent, grandparent, etc.

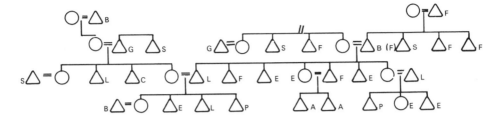

KEY:
L = Longshoremen, W = Logger, F = Farmer, B = Businessman (Owner),
T = Truckdriver, P = Professional, E = Semi-Professional, G = Police
or Fireman, A = Armed Forces Officer, S = Skilled Worker,
C = Construction Worker (Heavy Equipment Operator).

FIGURE 2   Detailed occupational genealogy of a longshoreman's family

Among the group of present day Portland longshoremen there are a number of men who previously held positions that fall within the last five categories. There are a fair number of longshoremen who were trained skilled workers and some still practice their previous trades in their spare time. Some came to the waterfront because they did not do well in their trades or because they had been rendered obsolete by a technological innovation. The most outstanding example of the latter category is a man who must have been one of the last trained in his trade, a butter barrel hoop maker who was displaced by the introduction of the steel barrel hoop. There are a number of trained school teachers, at least one ex-professor, and a medical doctor. There are also several one-time policemen and firemen who came to the waterfront for purely financial reasons. The list is extensive and there is no need to continue it here, because the pattern is apparent.

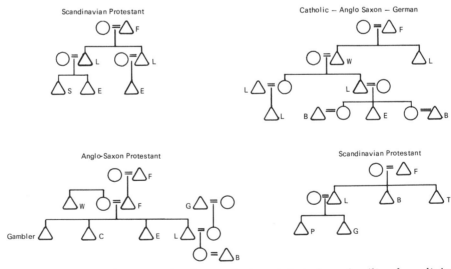

FIGURE 3   Sample occupational genealogies of longshore families by religion and ethnic affiliation

The occupations of the longshoremen's descendants and descendant collaterals* fall into the same six categories. Some occupations are noticeably absent from the list: there are few farmers and obsolete occupations such as horsetraders and blacksmiths. There are more professionals and semiprofessionals, more armed forces officers and fewer skilled workers, but again clerical and factory workers do not appear as male occupations. There is a somewhat higher level of educational attainment, but this is probably a reflection of the trend toward higher education in the nation as a whole.

The absence of clerical and factory workers is probably related to several factors. The longshoremen express a hearty disdain for both occupational categories, because they involve a regular nine to five work day and are thought to be insufficiently remunerative. Nor are they of a nature to support the longshoreman's claim to masculinity, since they lack the elements of extreme hazard and arduousness. Possibly the most important factors are those of selective migration to a frontier area and the occupational structure of the city and state. There is little need for clerical or factory workers in a frontier area, but there is a great need for craftsmen, the Jack-of-all-trades roughneck workers, certain kinds of professionals, and businessmen. As the area becomes less and less a frontier, the need for government workers and semiprofessionals increases proportionately. It is only with the growth of heavy manufacture that the need for clerical and semiskilled and unskilled workers reaches any critical level, but there is as yet little manufacture in Oregon. The largest manufacturing firm in the state produces complex electronic equipment which demands highly skilled workers and few others.

ASSOCIATION PATTERNS

There are three major bases of association in the longshore group; kinship, work and union, and special interest. Kinship is the most important of the three. The great majority of significant social relationships (primary) are with consanguineal or affinal kinsmen. Kinsmen are visited often even though they may live at some distance and are always felt to be closer than nonkin. The strong feeling toward kinsmen is displayed in mutual assistance such as helping to build a house, moving, or in financial aid. In one case a longshoreman traveled over eighty miles to help a brother-in-law refurbish rental property. Assistance in the form of voluntary manual labor is very frequent and small cash loans are made without question.

Much informal association takes place within the work and hiring hall contexts. Off-the-job association with other longshoremen accounts for nearly all nonfamily association although these two categories are difficult to separate because of the widespread kin ties among the longshoremen. Frequently, what appears to be a visit to another longshoreman turns out to be a visit to an affinal kinsman. This may contribute considerably to the feeling within the group that another longshoreman is a sort of kinsman. The same kinds of assistance are usually proffered

* Children, grandchildren, nephews and nieces, and cousins below the informant's generation level.

to unrelated longshoremen that are given to kinsmen. This seems to have been more prevalent in the past, but the growing affluence of the group and the formation of formal mechanisms for mutual assistance, such as the credit union and group insurance plans, have much reduced all forms of mutual assistance. To a lesser degree this has affected the frequency of mutual assistance between kinsmen.

The only significant basis for association outside of the longshore group seems to be special interests. These are fairly numerous, and there is no need to list them all, since a few examples will illustrate the pattern. The two best examples are the "rockhounds" and the motorcycle club. A rockhound is a person interested in the collection and display of various kinds of semiprecious stones and fossils. This activity demands a certain amount of training in geology and mineralogy and there is one man in the longshore group that has taken every relevant course taught within the state system of higher education. Both the rockhounds and the motorcycle enthusiasts invest a fair amount of time, energy, and money in their avocations, and, since the longshore group does not contain enough enthusiasts to maintain the appropriate clubs and associations, these men are members of larger groups composed for the most part of nonlongshoremen. Men are often recruited into the longshore group from such associations. They learn of the opportunity for waterfront employment from the longshore members of the club or association and thus enter into the longshore group.

The overall pattern is centered around the waterfront and longshore employment. The families tend to gain more and more longshore members by every conceivable combination of kin ties, and the special interest groups again tend to contribute members to the longshore group. What would appear to be a "centrifugal" force (association with outsiders) has in the end a "centripetal" or infolding effect. The activities in which most longshoremen engage that bring them into personal contact with outsiders are quite generally the sort of activities most likely to attract other perons very much like the longshoremen in terms of values and world-view, and these outsiders tend to be recruited into the longshore group. This holds true also for marriage outside the longshore group. First the association pattern extends to include new affinal kinsmen and then men from the affinal group tend to become longshoremen.

NATURE OF THE OCCUPATION

The nature of waterfront employment has changed a great deal since 1934, but it still has many undesirable features. The great irregularity of the work regime has been somewhat ameliorated by the union and the general improvement of the national economy in recent years, and mechanization has made the work easier, and stringent safety regulations enforced by the union and the federal and state governments have made it safer. Longshore work is nonetheless still irregular compared to other occupations, and is physically demanding and extremely hazardous. Few longshoremen have not been injured on the job and crippling and fatal injuries are all too frequent. I have witnessed two deaths that occurred on the job and have seen several men severely injured, not to mention innumerable minor injuries, and I have myself been hospitalized by injuries sustained while working on the waterfront. This is one of the sourecs of the "devil-may-care roughneck" image presented by the longshoremen: the physically dangerous nature of their work. Confidence in one's physical abilities and in the ability to remain calm in a crisis when the failure to act promptly and calmly could bring serious injury or death to oneself or one's fellow workers is essential to a longshoreman. Longshore work is extremely hazardous and longshoremen work in highly coordinated teams. Each member of the team depends on the other members not only to do their share of the work but to warn them of or protect them from impending danger. Consequently, one must not only have confidence in himself but he must be able to communicate this to other team members. Longshoremen are not alone in cherishing the image of the devil-may-care roughneck who always comes through in a crisis. He is a part of American folklore, epitomized in the dime novel heroes of the American frontier. The essential part of this role, however, is that the roughneck is always dependable and this image then contributes to alleviate the longshoremen's anxieties in the face of physical dangers and it also helps to alleviate his wife's anxieties concerning the family finances.

The arduous nature of longshore work demands workers who are physically tough and relatively strong. Although there is no statistical data available, my subjective impressions are that longshoremen are relatively large men. I stand 6′ 1″ in height and weigh about 195 pounds when in good trim, and although in most social groups I am nearly always one of the larger men, I am no more than average for the longshore group. The large size of the average longshoreman is undoubtedly related to their almost uniform North European ancestry, since North Europeans tend to be rather large; however, the ethnic composition of the city is almost identical with that of the longshore group, and the longshoremen tend to be significantly larger than most other Portlanders. Longshore work does not, however, demand such large men, and smaller men can and do work on the waterfront without undue hardship. The job really requires endurance rather than sheer strength, although great strength is certainly no handicap for a longshoreman, while the lack of a certain minimum of strength would be a severe disadvantage. For example, I once worked regularly with another longshoreman who, although he was considerably smaller than myself, was wiry and tough. When we were handling large heavy items such as 140 pound sacks of coffee, it was obvious that I felt considerably less physical strain than he; however, it was all I could do to keep pace with the rate at which he easily handled lighter commodities such as 50 pound sacks and cases of canned goods. The most plausible explanation for their large size is simply that large men are more likely to feel physically capable of performing the strenuous longshore work than are smaller, less muscular men (Buechley, et al., 1958).

Longshore work is also extremely demanding in other important ways. Each day a longshoreman must decide for himself whether or not he will go to work. He must balance economic necessity against the desire for leisure or extra-work activities. There is no goad to make him appear in the hiring hall to obtain employment other than economic necessity, since there are no penalties for not appearing in the hiring hall or for not working other than loss of pay. He must decide for himself how often he needs work, and the decision is his alone. If he is to earn a living for himself and his family, he must have a great deal of well developed self-discipline, which nearly all of the Portland longshoremen have. The lack of self-discipline could only lead to economic disaster. That the Portland longshoremen do accept sufficient employment is reflected in the earnings in Table 2 and in the savings deposits in the credit union. The deeply felt need for independence is what keeps the longshoreman on the waterfront. He is, of course, restricted by economic necessity, but he alone decides how to manage his financial affairs.

In response to the rhythm of waterfront employment where the harbor is either full of ships and there are not enough men to do the work or there are few or no ships and many men are idle, the longshoremen have developed what may be called a "feast-or-famine" philosophy. The core of this philosophy is that it is best to work when employment is plentiful and take one's leisure when it is scarce. In order to put this into practice, an individual must show up in the hall whenever there is a chance to obtain employment, which means almost every day. If he doesn't get a job, he can then engage in other activities. This of course only applies to those men who need a fairly high income and others may appear in the hall only three or four days per week.

On those days when work is not obtained, some of the longshoremen may sit in the basement recreation room of the hiring hall and play pinochle or poker. Some men will organize fishing expeditions, play golf, drink beer in a neighborhood tavern, simply go home and putter around the house, take their wives shopping or visiting, or drive around the countryside enjoying the scenery. A great deal of interaction with other longshoremen and their families takes place during these periods.

The irregularity of the work regime means that a longshoreman's wife seldom knows when her husband will be working, and owing to the uncertain length of the workshift, she is seldom certain when he will be home for supper. Planned days off only occur during long periods of high activity in the port, when the longshoremen have accumulated a fair surplus of ready cash. Even then, most of the men will schedule their days off so that they will not fall on the overtime days such as Saturday and Sunday when they are paid one and one-half times the normal pay scale, but will be absent from the waterfront on weekdays, when the premium rate does not apply.

Obviously, every family needs a certain minimum regular income and most of the longshoremen try to provide for short periods of unemployment by accumulating a certain amount of savings. The longshoremen's average pay is more than sufficient for his needs, but there are extended periods when work is short and, like other people everywhere, longshoremen have unexpected emergencies that demand ready cash. It was this need that was filled by the loan shark in the period between 1922 and 1934. The unlamented passing of the loan shark left a vacuum that was for a while filled by legitimate loan companies. Such loan companies, however, are distrustful of men who do not receive a steady salary or wage and it is often difficult for longshoremen to negotiate loans with them. Their interest rates, while not so high as those of loan sharks, are also rather steep. These problems were solved by the longshoremen with the establishment of a credit union in the early 1950s. The low interest rates and informality of the credit union made it an instant success and it has contributed significantly to the present affluence of the Portland longshoremen. The credit union will refinance a loan upon request and is slow to take formal action against a member in arrears. All of the paid employees are related to longshoremen and the board that makes the decisions as to whether or not to make a loan or move against a delinquent borrower is composed of longshoremen, who fully understand the needs and special problems of their fellows.

ATTITUDES TOWARD THE JOB

The Portland longshoremen do not conceive of themselves as employees but rather as union members and longshoremen. They never identify their occupation by saying that they work for some company or other. When questioned about their occupation by outsiders, they answer that they are longshoremen, that they work on the waterfront, or that they are members of the ILWU. This represents a considerable change from the 1922 to 1934 era, and is attributable to two major sources. Before 1934, the employers had attempted with some success to build an *esprit de corps* in their gangs (work crews) and among the other men who worked for them. They themselves were convinced that the men who worked in their "star" gangs were the best of all possible stevedores, and this built a sense of profession and pride of workmanship in the Portland longshoremen. Along with this the employers tried to establish a sense of loyalty to the company, but here they were less successful, possibly because of the pre-existing attitudes that had been engendered by previous union associations and affiliations.

Immediately after the strike in 1934, the union made a concerted effort to destroy forever whatever ties of loyalty had been developed between longshoremen and individual stevedore companies. At first this was a difficult task, especially with those men who had had preferred employment with a stevedore company or who had been regular dock employees and equipment operators, but the majority of the present longshoremen have never worked for any stevedore company or dock as regular or preferred employees. These men have worked out of the union operated hiring hall from the day that they first came to the waterfront, and feel absolutely no attachment to any company or to the waterfront employers in general. In fact, most of the younger men are openly hostile to the employers' representatives, whom they term "weasels."

The longshoreman's job is cherished both for the inherent qualities of the work, and for the freedom that it gives him. The nature of the shipping industry and the union and hiring system give the longshoreman a freedom of action available to very few other workers. He may come and go, work or not work as the mood and/or economic necessity move him. The work regime is always highly variable and the longshoreman may adjust his habits to fit the variable nature of the occupation, but he is never forced to punch a time clock or work on a rigid schedule. In addition the high pay is a powerful motivation and the view that longshoring is an extremely virile occupation is very important.

A young longshoreman.

THE MASCULINE IMAGE

That the longshoremen see their occupation as a proof of virility is evidenced in many ways, and cannot be discounted as an important factor in their motivation for working on the waterfront. This is often verbally expressed by the longshoremen, both directly and indirectly. Clerical and many other white-collar workers are often referred to in contemptuous terms ("Pencil Pusher," "Office Pinky") that clearly reflect the longshoremen's attitude that such work is clearly effeminate and only an effeminate male or one who was in some way inferior would resort to such employment. The sincerity of this attitude was recently put to the test in Portland with the opportunity for longshoremen to transfer to the ship's clerks (checker's) local (ILWU Local 40). The checkers resisted the attempts of longshoremen to transfer into their local, but the main reason that the resistance met with any success was that most of the longshoremen who applied for a transfer were not willing to put more than a token effort into the attempt.

Several men whose transfers would not have been resisted by the checkers made no attempt to transfer even though they had gained a good deal of experience at the work by taking extra checking jobs out of the longshore hall. Most of the men who had thus avoided becoming white-collar workers would or could not readily verbalize their reasons, but the gist of their statements was usually that it was just too much trouble. Nearly all were vaguely uneasy when discussing their motivations, and very vague in all of their statements. There would have been no loss of pay involved for any of these men, since checking pays exactly the same daily rate as longshoring and is exceptionally easy work, requiring little in the way of physical effort or educational skills. The only educational requirements are the ability to read and write English and to do simple arithmetic. Moreover, there is little or no loss of the longshoremen's cherished freedom, since the conditions of employment for checkers is again almost identical to that for longshoremen. The rejection of the job is based almost solely on the belief that it would do violence to their masculine self-image: it would not support their claim to virility in the same manner and degree that longshoring does.

PHYSICAL STRENGTH AND COURAGE

It does not seem surprising that men who work at hard and dangerous occupations should place a certain value on physical strength and courage, and it is essential that a longshoreman be relatively strong and possess a modicum of physical courage in order to endure the hardships and dangers of his everyday work. Confidence in one's physical abilities and the ability to remain calm in the presence of some degree of danger are absolutely essential in the longshore workplace, and the longshoremen do not leave this confidence behind when they leave their workplace. They often seem swaggering and overbearing to outsiders who encounter them in restaurants and business places, and their nonchalance when they encounter certain kinds of physical danger and their willingness to battle with their fists is often impressive and sometimes alarming to outsiders. They strongly believe that one should not flee from some relatively minor situation of threatening danger if there is any other alternative, and this has led to the popular impression that they are all too quick to use their fists in answer to a supposed slight or threat. As in all myths there is some truth in this. Longshoremen coming off the night shift at three o'clock in the morning are often welcomed in all night restaurants because of their willingness to restrain unruly intoxicated males who may be annoying the waitresses, as well as for their well-known propensity to spend a considerable amount on their meals.

The longshoremen in fact consider themselves real toughs and in no way effeminate or lacking in masculinity. They express great interest in masculine and strenuous sports such as boxing, wrestling, and football. On nights when an important game or boxing match, such as the contest for the heavyweight title is taking place, many of the longshoremen bring portable radios, and on some occasions, portable television sets, onto the job and all hands are kept informed of the contest's progress. On some of these events, there is fairly heavy wagering on the outcome and the supervision is aware that production will fall below normal expectations.

The men who engage in such sports are admired, and some athletes have been given waterfront employment, because they were well known local fighters or ball players. Underlying this kind of behavior is the belief that a man should be physically able, and have the courage to carry out his capabilities. This applies to perceived forms of courage and determination that do not involve physical danger or hardship. Under no circumstance should a man let himself be bullied or browbeaten by anyone who is not so much larger and more adept at fighting than himself that the chance of injuring his opponent does not exist.

How longshoremen define being "mean" to another man is interesting and sheds real light on their attitudes toward physical violence. The following narrative resulted when I asked an old-timer about another man who had been a member of the 1934 goon squad organization. I had implied that the other man perhaps enjoyed beating up on other men.

> Oh, he liked to raise a little bit of hell or anything, but he was far from a bully. There's not a mean streak in—the only time I ever seen him get mean was with young _____, and one night he was working at Terminal Four and I believe it was after that first M and M [modernization and mechanization] contract we signed. And they were all bitching about it. And he and I was sitting in there eating our lunch, and young _____ came in with two or three other of those young guys, and he's talking like that. And he started in on young _____. You see we knew his dad; we both knew his dad. It is the only time I ever seen him really browbeat a guy. But _____ had it coming; he had quite a bit of browbeating coming. But it's about the meanest I ever seen him get. But it's the only time I ever seen him browbeat a guy.

The implications of this may be obvious, but some elaboration may be helpful. It was in this case meaner to browbeat the young man because it totally stripped him of his dignity. The younger man was faced by a man he could not beat in a fist fight and thus did not dare challenge. He was forced to display his fear through his inaction while being browbeaten. It would have been a kinder move to have knocked him down.

An older longshoreman.

This cluster of beliefs leads to the learning of combative skills and attitudes early in life, in order that one may not have to be humiliated as was the young man in the case just cited. Usually such skills are learned in working-class schools where the boys tend to engage in much more fighting than in middle-class neighborhoods. This fighting is encouraged by their fathers, and they are also taught to fight in formal situations. In almost all cases, a certain amount of instruction is received from the boy's father, who usually feels a responsibility to teach him to fight efficiently enough that he will not be disgraced in neighborhood scraps. The outcome of this training is that most longshoremen are not only somewhat more willing to engage in physical conflict, but are also capable of doing so in a relatively competent fashion.

That the accent on courage is not mere bravado is evidenced by the military record of the longshore group. The longshoremen feel obliged to do military service and many volunteer before they are drafted in order to be able to pick the branch of the service in which they will serve. Interestingly, the number of men who have chosen their branch of the service have most often chosen to serve in combat outfits such as the Marine Corps, Army Infantry, Paratroops, and underwater demolitions teams. The number of men who have served in such organizations in actual combat is also rather high. There are men in the longshore group who have taken part in almost every battle fought by American troops in World War II and the Korean War. For example, there is one longshoreman who was in the Bataan Death March, and another who was a member of the first underwater demolitions team (frogmen) organized by the United States Navy.

Related to these attitudes is the belief that force is a legitimate and sometimes the only means of settling some disputes. Violence in the form of fighting with the fists is thought to be the most appropriate response to an offense to one's dignity or integrity. Consequently, verbal insults are more likely to evoke violence from a longshoreman than from many other people. Unfavorable references to sexual behavior, to the morals of the longshoreman or any member of his family or a friend, insults offered to a woman, remarks that might be interpreted to imply a lack of courage or of proper union principles are all thought to be properly answered with physical violence and usually are. Violence is not thought to be an appropriate response to a disagreement over union policy or affairs, but the lofty goal of nonviolent settlements is not always attained. Fights have occurred in union meetings and over union affairs frequently enough that the union has taken serious measures to bring them to an end, but challenges to battle are still, although less frequently, issued. Fights resulting from conflict within the union meetings are quite rare, but although I have not seen or heard of a fight in the hall itself in many years, occasionally a dispute is thus settled in the parking lot or elsewhere.

It is not thought unusual for a young man to indulge in fighting, even to what must seem an excessive degree to outsiders, so long as he does not make a nuisance of himself within the group. Some men do, however, carry this activity further than most of the longshoremen care for, and sooner or later such persons are dealt with by some member of the group. One man who had been somewhat of a bully and had gained a bad reputation for excessive quarrelsomeness was humiliated by having his head thrust into a toilet bowl and the toilet duly flushed by another longshoreman. Another large, powerful and quite rotund individual knocked the same offender through a plate glass window by striking him with his belly. It is quite clear that such activities cannot be carried out too long because such pugnaciousness is bound to be challenged many times, and sooner or later the offender is certain to be beaten and perhaps humiliated.

Fighting is invariably done with the fists, and the use of a weapon except in response to an armed assault is thought not only to be unfair but an expression of cowardice. This practice differs widely from that of some of the Eastern ports and many other parts of the world, but it is common to the area: fighting with weapons is not regarded as appropriate by any of the roughneck elements of the Pacific Northwest. To my knowledge, the only form of fighting involving weapons at any time in this area was the use of caulk boots by loggers (lumberjacks), and this practice is long extinct.

Fighting or "battling," as it is usually referred to, follows a set of formalized rules familiar to most fans of that great American art, the western movie. These are the essentials of fair play as epitomized by John Wayne. As stated above, all battling should be done with the fists between adversaries of approximately equal prowess. Bullying a smaller or older man is forbidden by the rules, as is carrying a grudge after the battle is over. The rules are, of course, violated, but the disapproval of the social group is intense on these occasions. On the other hand, a man gathers to himself the respect of the other men if he is able to either lose or win a fight in good style.

Two incidents, one that I observed and one that I was told about, should illustrate this point. On one occasion, a company superintendent who had risen from the ranks of the longshoremen and had a reputation for being a good man with his fists took it upon himself to berate a gang that was working in the hold of a freighter. He loudly informed them from the top deck that they were slacking and roughly ordered them to start working. Their joint reply was the usual waterfront reply to such an order couched in powerful Anglo-Saxon obscenities. He took offense at this reply and stated that he "could lick any man in the gang," which was something of a boast considering that although he was hard and in good shape he was almost sixty years of age. One of the men in the gang replied instantly that this was not true and never had been, whereupon he was invited by the superintendent to step out onto the dock and test his hypothesis. The younger man was about thirty years the superintendent's junior, about the same size and build, and had fought professionally for a short period. The outcome was predictable: the younger man floored the superintendent with his first punch. This could have resulted in a great deal of trouble for the younger man, but the superintendent, who had never felt alienated from the longshore group and had been raised with its code of ethics, simply said, "All right, you won, let's go back to work." By doing so he greatly enhanced his reputation among the other longshoremen as a man of principle as well as courage. In other words, he was "a real man."

During the 1934 strike, a riot squad under the command of one of the most respected battlers on the waterfront, set out to beat up a foreman who had been working behind the picket lines. He was found on the street and the squad commander sent a very large young man to beat up the foreman, who was well past his prime. The younger man met with little success because the old foreman put up a good fight by using his leather briefcase as a weapon. As the riot squad commander reported it to me,

> That big young punk should have been able to floor the old man with one punch, because he was big enough to go bear hunting with a switch. And the old man beat him off with that little old briefcase and he started to squeal for help. Well, I was so disgusted that I told him, "I hope he licks you," and we drove off.

In this case the young goon lost status in the eyes of his peers not so much because he failed to bring the old strikebreaker down, but because he asked for help against a relatively harmless opponent. On the other hand, the strikebreaker was accorded a grudging respect because he had put up a good fight against odds.

A few men were also involved, after the strike was settled, in driving out men who had scabbed when they tried to return to work. Their method was simply to wait in the hiring hall until an ex-strikebreaker came in and then they would beat him up and tell him never to appear there again. In most cases, this tactic was quite successful, but one or two of these men kept coming back to try to go to work despite the beatings, and the strong arm men gave up the attempt to discourage them. One of these men told me that he just "didn't have the heart to hit the poor bastards again." Despite the fact that he felt that these men deserved to be beaten and driven off, in these few cases, he felt he was coming too close to being a bully.

TRAVEL AND COSMOPOLITANISM

The involvement with military service has helped to produce a well-traveled and rather sophisticated group of males. A great many of the men have served overseas in the armed forces, and some of them have traveled widely. Partially because of this and to some degree because of the number of longshoremen who were merchant seamen or led transient lives, traveling from place to place and earning only enough to travel a little further, when they were young men (traditionally known as going on the tramp), there are few of the Portland longshoremen who have not traveled around the United States, and a significant number of them have seen a good deal of the world. Their experience with persons other than Americans is extensive and gives them a sophistication concerning other lands and other peoples that seems unusual for a group of working men in a small western city. Certainly, they seem more sophisticated in such matters than most of the other citizens of Portland. Moreover, contact with sailors from all parts of the world is a daily occurrence for longshoremen, and these day-to-day contacts provide men who have acquired foreign languages an opportunity to exercise these skills, as well as to continue a relationship with the people of countries with which they have become familiar. This contact with foreign sailors also provides those longshoremen who are not widely traveled the chance to come in contact with representatives of countries they have never had the opportunity to visit, and thus to develop some understanding of these peoples and their varied ways of life.

3 / The union: history and development

The Portland Local of the International Longshoremen's and Warehouse-men's Union (Local 8) is the most central of the institutions that serve to integrate the longshore community. The history of the development of the union is very much the history of the development of the community. It not only brought the aggregation of longshoremen together into a coherent group, but it was also explicitly designed to offset the special problems of waterfront employment through rank-and-file union control of the hiring and dispatch systems, and of the recruitment and control of the pool of regular longshoremen. The attempts of previous unions and employer-controlled hiring systems to exclude corruption and equalize work opportunity among the longshoremen had universally failed. This union designed itself so as not to inherit the weaknesses of its predecessors. That they were successful in this monumental task is the consequence of both historical conditions and processes and of the particular cluster of men who formed the core of the new union. It must be borne in mind that this union was formed during a tremendous wave of unionization throughout the country fostered by Section 7 of the National Recovery Act which lifted the weight of the provisions of the Sherman Act from the unions: it gave them the right to engage in "collective action" which means "strike" in the language of unions.

THE 1922 STRIKE

One of the most significant years in the history of the Portland waterfront was 1922, because it brought the end of craft unionism and cleared the way for the development of industrial unionism. The strike had been long in the making. The Waterfront Employers' Union had been gathering its forces with the avowed intent of breaking the longshoremen's union (ILA Local 6) since 1919 (Waterfront Employers' Union, 1919). The union had two internal weaknesses that greatly influenced later events. First, the number of union men who were preferentially hired—that is, hired before nonunion men—was less than one fourth of the regular longshore work force. The second weakness was that recruitment into the union was on a strict "brother-in-law" basis: a prospective longshoreman had to be a relative, lodge brother, or very close friend of a union member in order to have any hope of ever entering the union. Nonunion men were regularly assigned to the hardest work after the union members had taken the easier jobs. With a union membership of about 250 men, the nonunion work force that was regularly hired out of the ILA hall was around 800. Many of these men were not relatives of union members, and consequently stood little chance of ever becoming union members. Among them there was a significant number of Wobblies (Industrial Workers of the World), and almost none of them were related to ILA members.

When the Waterfront Employers' Union (later the Waterfront Employers' Association) forced the longshoremen out on strike (WEU, 1921, 1922), many of the nonunion men crossed the ILA picket lines and went to work. Very noticeably almost all of the Wobblies were nonstrikers. Their bitterness at being excluded from the ranks of the ILA had found an outlet in the strike, and when attempts were made after the strike was lost to work ILA and IWW men on the same ship, the situation became tense and then broke into open violence.

Before the 1922 strike, the ILA had had a hiring hall from which most of the Portland longshoremen were dispatched and the employers' opening move was to start up a hiring hall of their own patterned after the employers' hall in Seattle (Larrowe 1955). After the strike all Portland longshoremen were hired out of the employers' hall and the union hall was closed. The old situation had been reversed. The Wobblies were now the first and the ILA men the last to be hired. It would, of course, be an error to say that all or even most of the strike-breakers were Wobblies, but many were, and this fact laid the basis for many of the events of 1933. After the 1922 strike there were no effective unions on the Portland waterfront or elsewhere on the Pacific coast, except in Tacoma, Washington, and there is some question as to the actual effectiveness of the Tacoma ILA Local. The employers ruled the waterfront with a free hand, and the union was completely destroyed. Most of the men who had belonged to the ILA felt they had no chance to reorganize and were unwilling to take a chance against odds.

"FINK HALL"

The employers' hiring hall in Portland (dubbed Fink Hall by the longshoremen) was originally intended to function in the same manner as the one in Seattle. Union and nonunion men were to be dispatched from the hall without preference or discrimination (Buchanan 1964). This did not, however, take place, and union men were discriminated against from the outset and several other unintended activities began with the institution of the employers' hall. The first unforeseen event was that two stevedore companies left the Waterfront Employers' Union, and, claiming that they were not being sent gangs as they ordered them, set up their own hiring hall (the Little Hall) less than a block away (Personal Communication, Portland Stevedore, 1923).

In both halls, the discretion to hire or not to hire a particular man or gang was usually left in the hands of the hiring hall dispatchers and the gang bosses. Gangs would be ordered for jobs and the hiring slips (pads) would be given to the gang bosses who would then go out into the hall and pick out the men to fill in their gangs. There were no regular rules for dealing with who should or should not be hired, and it soon became obvious to many of the men that both the gang bosses and the dispatchers could be influenced in their favor by gifts of money or liquor or by performing certain services for them. Also, because of the irregular nature of the work, the longshoremen were often in need of money, and the ubiquitous loan shark soon made an appearance. The loan sharks also found that they could influence the dispatchers with gifts and thus influence the hiring. One man even had an office in the waterfront Employers' Union's hall. It was sometimes advantageous to a longshoreman to owe money to certain of these loan sharks, because he would see to it that the longshoreman obtained at least enough employment to pay his debt. I have been told that some men didn't collect their own pay for months at a time. The "brother-in-law" system of recruitment was soon reinstated. Friends and relatives of the gang bosses and dispatchers could nearly always find employment on the waterfront. For these men, pay-offs and kickbacks were usually unnecessary, and networks of kinship became widespread throughout the longshore group.

ILA Local 6 had maintained an eight-hour day and worked no overtime, but with employer control of the hiring process the work day was often extended considerably. The official work shift was still eight hours, but shifts of 36 hours and more were not uncommon in periods of peak activity. The speed-up was immediately instituted, and men who objected either to the long hours or to the pace of work were reportedly told to leave if they were unhappy with the job. Men who did leave in this fashion were blackballed in the hiring halls and were unable to regain waterfront employment.

ETHNIC COMPOSITION OF THE GROUP

Information on the ethnic composition of the longshore group prior to 1934 is difficult to obtain, because no records from that period are available. Indirect means must be used to obtain an indication, and only an indication, of the ethnic composition of the Portland longshoremen between 1922 and 1934. Three kinds of evidence may be followed. First, the ethnic composition of the population of the state indicated that most of the residents of Oregon were native-born Americans of North European ancestry and that about a third of the total population were native Oregonians. The second line of evidence consists of an analysis of the surnames of men on the deceased pensioners' list maintained by the present longshoremen's union. This will not tell us where these men were born, but it will give a rough idea of their ethnic origins. This analysis shows that in round figures 44% of the deceased pensioners bore Anglo-Saxon surnames, 33% Scandinavian, 18% German, and only 5% all others. This set of figures shows clearly that the ethnic backgrounds of this group of Portland longshoremen, even allowing for a fair amount of error, was almost completely North European. How many were native Americans is not indicated. The third line of evidence consists of statements made by informants, and the backgrounds of living men who were in the Portland longshore group during the period in question. Here the indication is that many of the Scandinavians were immigrants, not from Scandinavia, but from Wisconsin, Minnesota, and the Dakotas. This is borne out by some of the literature dealing with migration into Oregon (Pollard 1951 and Bjork 1958). Again, many of the longshoremen bearing German surnames were from Pennsylvania-Dutch and other German-American backgrounds. Upon questioning, many of these men cannot say when their ancestors entered the United States, but it was clearly more than four generations in the past.

That many of the Portland longshoremen were foreign-born cannot, however, be denied, but the proportion was probably not over 30% at any time, and this is undoubtedly a liberal estimate. The conclusions about the ethnic composition of the longshore group between 1922 and 1934 that can reasonably be drawn are: first, the ultimate origin of nearly all of the men was North European; second, the majority of the men were native Americans; third, many of the men were native Oregonians; and fourth, there was a large minority of foreign-born, predominantly Germans and Scandinavians.

STATUS CATEGORIES

The longshore group was divided into two main categories by the employers, and these categories are seen as significant by many of my informants. The categories were concerned with gang membership. Before 1922, there had been no regular organized gangs (work crews), but the employers' association organized the longshoremen into cargo gangs as soon as they had set up their hiring hall. Gangs were identified by their work functions. Some were steel gangs, log gangs, lumber gangs, and general cargo gangs. These gang men were the employers' handpicked men, often referred to as "star" men by the longshoremen. It is doubtful whether the entire category of gang men constituted any sort of meaningful social group, because each gang was normally employed by one company and its members seldom worked with men who worked for other companies. The gang men had higher and more regular earnings than the "hall men" who were hired to fill in when the gangs needed extra men. Smaller social groups existed among men who worked for the same company and many of the association patterns established at that time still exist among some of the present day Portland longshoremen.

The majority of gang men maintained stable families and were relatively steady workers. As previously indicated, many of these men were related and the degree of relationship steadily increased with time. The preferential recruitment of relatives was, however, only one factor in the increasing ramification of longshore kinship networks. Many affinal ties developed simply because the longshoremen often visited each other's homes and met the families of their associates. At one point when I was interviewing an old-time longshoreman concerning the hiring practices of this period, the informant delivered a tirade against the selective recruitment of longshore kin (the "brother-in-law" system), and shortly thereafter was rather embarrassed when he was forced to admit that his own brother-in-law was also a longshoreman. This relationship was not attributable to the "brother-in-law" system, however, but simply to the fact that one longshoreman had married another longshoreman's sister.

The "hall men" constituted the second category of longshoremen during this period. Not as homogeneous a group as the gang category, it was again split into two subcategories. First, there was a larger number of men who would rather have been gang men, and who were very like the gang men in their social life and activities. However, they lacked the approval of the employers, dispatchers, and gang bosses and so for one reason or another could not become regular gang men. Some were barred for union activities, others because they were not able to keep up the frantic pace of the work, and yet others because they had incurred the enmity of some influential person or group of persons. These men may have formed a more coherent social group than the gang men because of their more frequent association with one another in the hiring hall context, but there is little evidence to indicate that this is so.

The second category of hall men was a varied group indeed, and can in no sense of the word be called a social group. These men, according to my informants, were for the most part only seeking a "visible means of support" and not attempting to earn a living on the waterfront. They were thieves, drifters, pimps, and con men of every variety, as well as men who had failed in some other occupation and who had simply become drifters. At most they wanted a few days' work at infrequent intervals so that they could say they were longshoremen when the police questioned them or so that they could drift on a little further or buy one more bottle of booze. These are the men mentioned earlier that Barnes (1915) called "shenangoes." They really were not longshoremen and further references to hall men will not include them. They are, however, of some significance in that they are a major source of the longshoreman's deplorable public image. They were described in the following manner by an old-time longshoreman.

> When I first started on the Portland waterfront there were more derelict men than I've ever seen accumulated together in my life. There were people like Broadway Johnny and Brute Carson—there's one or two still living. But they were—they all had girls and they had to have a visible means of support. So they hung around the waterfront because there was crap games and there was poker games and we could connive a little bit this way and that. And you take it all and all, there really weren't 150 men [out of a group of about 600 men] that were actually working out of that hall for a living. To the others it was more of a meeting place.

ADAPTATIONS TO THE NATURE OF THE WORK

The motivation of most of the longshoremen for seeking waterfront employment was freedom from a rigid work regime. Although the Waterfront Employers' Association boasted of the efficiency and dependability of their gang men, there are indications that many of their men were prone to take a day off when the spirit moved them. Perhaps these men had some sort of protection provided by friends or relatives in influential positions, because many old-timers have told me that if they had not shown up when ordered on a job, they would have been black-balled. Nevertheless, the nature of the work is such that the work regime could not have been very regular at any time.

It is also true that many of the longshoremen, both hall and gang men, had sources of income other than the waterfront. The "stump rancher," a man who works a small farm on logged-off land, seems to be a Northwestern institution. Some men held other part-time jobs and some conducted small business opera-tions. In any case, there were times when it was difficult to make a steady living as a longshoreman, even as a member of a preferred gang. A small subsistence farm contributes a significant amount of income during such periods, and after the land is completely cleared, it may be subdivided and sold as building sites or devel-oped into a profitable business—that is, a paying farm. Small-time entrepreneurial activities of other kinds were also among the economic activities of some of the longshoremen. Land owning, then as now, was a high value in the regular long-shore group, and some longshoremen realized a steady income from rentals.

NATURE OF THE MEN

The educational level of the Portland longshoremen in the 1920s was rather low as is indicated by the fact that a number of them were illiterate. Exactly how they compared with the rest of the population is impossible to say due to lack of comparative statistical data, and because illiteracy was not uncommon at that time. There were, however, a few men with college degrees and one medical doctor among the longshoremen.

The longshoremen of this period were well-known as "two-fisted" fighters and drinkers. A longshoreman had to be a fair physical specimen in order to carry out the arduous labor demanded of him on the job, and as one informant stated, "Timid men don't work on the waterfront." Fights on the waterfront were not rare, and a man was expected to defend himself if attacked or to fight if challenged. Never-theless, it is extremely doubtful that all of the longshoremen engaged in as many fist fights as the legends would indicate. However, Portland was a rough town in the years between 1923 and 1933, and it was the chief recreation area for the young unmarried loggers, sawmill workers, construction workers, and longshoremen who made up most of the local work force. The staid Portland of today bears little re-semblance to the "wide open" town of the twenties where Chinese gambling estab-lishments were ubiquitous and where the local ladies of ill repute dangled their stock in trade from their hotel windows on a Sunday morning in order to attract extra revenue. It must be borne in mind that Oregon was very much a recent fron-tier area at this time with all that that implies in terms of behavior, even though the state was never characterized by the violence that marked the history of Wash-ington and California and much of the West.

The longshoremen did not identify themselves primarily as union men or long-shoremen but rather as employees of certain companies or as members of certain gangs. The hall men may have been more given to seeing themselves simply as longshoremen but evidence for this is lacking. Many of the union men, both ILA and IWW, still remained on the waterfront and the union ideologies never died out; but an extensive network of company spies and the blackball system effectively discouraged most of them from trying to reorganize the port or to improve the conditions under which they worked. Attempts at organization were made from time to time, but all were abortive until 1933 (Buchanan 1964 and Larrowe 1955). Most of the men kept working and said little, but they did not like the conditions under which they worked or the corruption of the hiring system. They were, in fact, extremely bitter about the humiliations to which they were forced to submit in order to remain on the waterfront, and this bitterness was to add to their determination in the conflict of 1934.

PATTERN OF IMMIGRATION

The ethnic composition of the basic longshore group and the population of Portland has been outlined, but there are certain other aspects of the pattern of immigration that greatly affected the attitudes of the longshoremen and the citizens of Portland. Most of the migrants were native Americans, but they did not represent a random sampling of the more settled parts of the United States. The first American immigrants tended to be from the New England states and the South. Many of the notable early settlers were from Tennessee and the Carolinas. But after the establishment of the transcontinental railways in 1883 (Pollard 1951) there was a vast wave of migration from the Midwest. The total population of the state increased almost four times between 1880 and 1910, and it is with the people of Oregon as an importantly Midwestern population that we must deal. Those who came over the Oregon trail in covered wagons were the more colorful group, but the immigrants who came in railroad coaches were by far the more important in determining the character of the longshore group.

ORIGINS OF THE UNION IDEOLOGY

The midwestern states were hotbeds of Populism (a left-wing political ideology advocating agrarian reform, the free coinage of silver, and government control of monopolies) in this period and it is not surprising to find that Oregon was soon an area in which Populism was not an uncommon political viewpoint. The "Oregon system" of direct legislation is but one of the results of the Populist movement in Oregon. As Oregon ceased being a completely open frontier area with the arrival of the Midwestern immigrants, the industrial and consequently the occupational structure of the state changed considerably. Most of the people in Oregon had been in agriculture. Now the spectrum was changing toward industrial occupations, primarily in the timber and service industries.

In the East, the assembly line factory with its demand for a huge and unskilled labor army was just coming into being. The need for unskilled labor was met by the wave of foreign immigration from Ireland and the countries of Southern and

Eastern Europe. Eastern industry wanted cheap labor to perform tasks that could be taught to anyone in a matter of minutes. There was no large group of deprived native American workers to fill this need. The vast majority of American workers were either craftsmen of one kind or another or farmers, and many of them went west as the waves of foreign migrants entered the industrialized urban areas of the East and Midwest.

The native American workers in no sense represented a proletariat. Where they remained in the industrial centers they formed an elite of skilled workers often represented by craft unions. Many of them went west and some settled in Oregon where their skills were needed. Many native American farmers also migrated to Oregon. Some founded farms and ranches and prospered; many others went into the woods and there earned the "stake" needed to set themselves up in business or to buy land. There is one outstanding similarity in all of these people: they were all seeking economic advancement, greater opportunities in business. There has never been anything resembling a peasant in the northern part of the United States. American farmers are businessmen and bear a great resemblance to most craftsmen in that they do or did most of their own labor. They were men who worked with their hands, and to them such work bore no stigma.

To the early lumber barons, however, labor was just labor and to be exploited as much as possible. This was not palatable to the Midwesterner raised in a tradition of personal independence and pride, and the close association of these people with Populism made them more than susceptible to the syndicalist theories of the Industrial Workers of the World. The challenge of the lumber magnates was swiftly met in the sawmills and lumber camps of the Northwest by the Wobblies who were concentrated in the ranks of loggers and timber workers. In the early part of the twentieth century the Northwest was still something of a frontier area. Law and order were difficult to maintain and in some places organizations, such as the Commercial Club of Everett, Washington, used vigilantes to police their workers. The Western IWW met these tactics with their own version of terror and concerted campaigns of sabotage. In Oregon, on the other hand, quite unlike the rest of the Pacific coast, there was very little of this kind of violence, which may well be the result of the near homogeneity of the population and which was most certainly conditioned by the political structure of the state.

Portland was very much a timber workers' town, and many loggers and sawmill workers, tiring of their vagabond life, settled in the city. The loggers' skills were not useful in every trade, but they were most certainly useful on the waterfront where much of the cargo shipped out of the port consisted of logs and lumber products. Loggers were also familiar with rigging and gear of much the same type used on ships. Thus, there have always been many ex-loggers among the Portland longshoremen, and those loggers were one of the chief sources of the left-wing ideology that so permeates the union.

4/The union: the 1934 strike

The 1934 strike was much more than a labor dispute. It was part of a social revolution that was sweeping the country. The country was in the throes of the great depression, and the laws that allowed unions the right to strike were a part of the economic policy of the New Deal. Workmen's compensation, unemployment insurance, and social security were among the many changes in the national milieu instituted by the government in its attempts to alleviate the human problems of the depression. But to the Portland longshoremen, the 1934 strike was a revolution on a local and much more personal level than the events of the national scene. Deeply imbued with the ideals of Populism and syndicalism, they saw the opportunity to create for themselves the sort of union that could put these ideals into practice. The Communists also contributed to this set of ideals primarily because they were so close to the other left-wing ideologies, and because the Communist party afforded the structure through which coast-wide organization was achieved by the Union. Another sort of revolution was also involved in this strike: the revolt of proud and independent men who had had to submit to personal humiliation in order to support themselves and their families, and they entered into the fray with a vengeance.

By 1932, the Portland waterfront was in the complete control of the Waterfront Employers' Association; however, their ranks had split and there were in effect two associations competing with one another, each with its own hiring hall and its own regular men and gangs. But the employers were still in complete control, and no union had arisen to challenge their supremacy. Several attempts at organization had failed in the past decade and they felt secure in their position, and the majority of the longshoremen concurred with the employers' opinion. There had, however, been a continuing subrosa union organizing campaign. This campaign had used many of the techniques of an underground or spy organization. Men who had joined the union or pledged to join were not known even to one another. This level of secrecy had been necessary because of the labor spies used by the employers, and because any man who joined the union and became known as a union member was sure to be blackballed. The Depression aided the union campaign. Competition became extremely severe among the shipping and stevedore companies, and the only way they could compete with one another was to push the men harder, trying to get more production at the same cost. In addition, they had cut the hourly rate received by longshoremen.

In 1933, the National Industrial Recovery Act was passed by Congress. Section 7 (A) of this act guaranteed unions the right to organize and gave the union members protection from the blackball system (Cox and Bok 1965). The organizers of the longshoremen's union, most of whom were former members of the IWW, accelerated their efforts, combined with the organizational efforts of the rest of the Pacific coast longshoremen, and went out on strike when San Francisco gave the word on May 9th, 1934. (For details of the pre-strike and strike period see Buchanan 1964 and Larrowe 1955.)

UNION DEMANDS

The most important features of the longshoremen's demands were a concern with the hiring procedures, union recognition, and the length of the work day. Recognition of the Union and virtual union control of the hiring process were extremely important. In a semicasual occupation like longshoring, the closed shop is an absolute necessity to any sort of effective unionism. Otherwise the union may be disposed of by simply bringing in more and more nonunion men until there are enough to do the work and the union men are effectively out of a job. Control of the hiring process is also essential to the existence of the union, because the same procedure can be used to remove the union, through discriminatory practices in the hiring hall—hiring nonunion in preference to union men. The corruption of the hiring process had aroused real bitterness among the longshoremen as had the "slave driver" tactics used by foremen on the job. Control of the hiring hall meant the end of this corruption, a point that will be described in a later section on the hiring system, and it meant that the blackball system could be brought to an end. The demand to bring the working day down to six hours straight time was an attempt to spread the work around among the men who had been badly hurt by the drop in shipping caused by the Depression and also contained an element of revenge against the employer for the brutally long work shifts that had been demanded of the longshoremen during the period of employer control.

Many of the longshoremen were truly afraid to join the union or to strike because of the pattern of defeat that had been established over the years. Others, men who held key positions, were afraid of losing their "soft" jobs. Some of these men continued to work during the strike, either from fear or because they expected to gain some advantage from their demonstrated loyalty to the employers. Many of the strikers also believed they could not win, but, as many have told me, they believed that they had nothing more to lose. In many cases they thought that it would be better to be forced off the waterfront than to continue the brutal and degrading labor that was their lot under the conditions imposed by the waterfront employers.

WORKING CONDITIONS

The conditions under which these men worked are unbelievable by modern standards. Shifts of over thirty-six hours were common, and if a man protested,

Picket squad on duty during 1934 strike. (Photo by Toby Christensen)

he could be quite sure that he would never work on the waterfront again. One old-timer described these conditions in this manner:

> They would hire their gangs and you would be on that dock at seven o'clock Tuesday morning. And maybe that ship would get in at nine o'clock Tuesday night. But you didn't dare leave. You were hired but you weren't getting paid. And there you sat. And you talked and shot crap and did this and you did that. And then when the ship came, you went aboard and you worked her out [stay aboard and work until the ship was completely loaded or unloaded and ready to sail]. Sometimes you'd have a fifteen minute lunch break, sometimes when they really wanted to sail her, they'd throw sandwiches down in the hold. One time we worked eight hours between eating—we worked eight hours without breakfast or anything else, because they kept saying, "fifty more ton, fifty more ton, fifty more ton." And you've only got to say that four or five times and it stretches into hours.

Another man described the conditions in this manner.

> It got so bad up to '34, it got so bad, they didn't care whether you went to eat or not. Didn't—you had your noon meal—they usually let you have that. But from there on they didn't care whether you ate or not. I have worked on the *Rose City*. Went to work at eight in the morning, I have worked all day, I

have worked all night, I have worked till noon the next day to finish the ship. All day, all night, until noon the next day. And I've worked many a time on the paper boats all day, all night, and had the boss to holler from the top of the hatch, "Go to breakfast and be back at eight o'clock."

PERSONAL RELATIONS

Relations among the men and between the men and the companies was accurately and incisively described by another man in this manner.

Now my understanding of relationships on the front: first, the men were in direct competition; there was no system of hiring. The walking bosses would come in the hall at certain times, that is, 7:30 a.m., 11:30 a.m., and at 4:30 p.m. If you wanted a job, you had to be there these three times a day or till you got on. Now if you will think, you can easily see that in the competition for the jobs—and remember that many times it meant the difference in how much one had to eat—it was "dog eat dog." Men would do most anything to get the job including giving kickbacks. I chided one boss who had lost his job about taking things for giving men jobs, and he said that he did not get any money, but did find many pints in the gear locker. He did more than that, however. I had worked for this man for two years regularly, and the only thing I ever gave him was to laugh at his bum jokes. The reason that he hired me was because I was about the age that you [the author] are, and strong and willing, but, if I had ever started giving him anything then I would have had to keep it up or else. So we were in a vicious circle, all of us, including the employers. They had an organization, but only to fight us, or, as they saw it, to protect theirselves against the men. The real employers, those that had the money, never saw us, did not know us and did not want to. They hired managers, superintendents, foremen and so on, whose only job was to bring them profits. So it was their job to drive us. They could be slave drivers or slaves. And the employers cut each other's throats underbidding each other for the contracts, the same as we did by working harder to get the jobs or giving kickbacks for the same reason.

ROLE OF THE WOBBLIES

The IWW's did not have official control of the local when the strike was called. The membership had elected officials who were associated with craft unionism, and these men held the key posts in the local until 1937 when the Portland longshoremen left the ILA. On the other hand, the most active and influential members of the local were the men of IWW persuasion and background. It was they who actually led the strike, planned the tactics and strategies, and led the men. One of the old Wobblies, a very important man in the organization of the Local, related the confusion and emerging order of the first day of the strike in the following manner. His first remarks refer to the confusion and lack of experience of the top officials of the Local.

The first day the strike come on these guys never had any experience or a cock-eyed thing. I was making all the contacts around, and they didn't know really what I was doing. They weren't interested. And so I know the night before the strike I said, "All right now, you guys are going to call the guys off on the strike tomorrow. Now what are you going to do with them when you get them out?" I said, "Had you planned on feeding them? How're you going to dispatch pickets . . . you got any plans for that?" They didn't have a goddamn thing. I worked for the executive board—they all were, you know—not a goddamned plan. I said, "Do you think that's the way you run the strike? Just call a strike, boom, and that takes care of it?" I said, "That's where you lost your ass in the past. You're not going to do it this time." And, well, "What would I suggest?" I said, "Well," I said, "Tomorrow morning things are pretty much going to take care of themselves. We wouldn't have any chance for any orderly deal like dispatches for pickets and all that—what the hell, pickets are going to be all over the place anyway. It's going to be a mob." You couldn't control them, you couldn't dispatch them. You couldn't do anything—I knew that. And it worked out that way too. Jesus. But the way to get them, I tell you, was—I got down early that morning. I was down so early that the only people around there was two parked cars full of plainclothesmen parked a block from the—I knew, I knew—that they were cops. I don't say I knew them individually. I knew they were cops. And so I looked in, and I said, "You guys are out kinda early, aren't you?" "It looks to me like you are," one of them said. I said, "Oh, I have a reason to be out early. I work down here. What do you do?" "Oh, we just thought we'd sit around for a while." "Well, you do that," I says. And pretty soon along come three more—four more guys that I had contacted the night before. Now, the thing that no one knew was how many men belonged to the union. Hell, I used to have to chase them when—you know, when they were having to piss —to organize them. I talked to a lot of them who would be afraid to be seen talking to me, you know. Now this thing worked out all right, because of that, see. And so you'd be working with the guy next to you and you didn't know whether he was in the union or not—he wasn't going to tell you because he was afraid you might go ahead and tell Jack O'Neal. So anyway, I used that kind on them—little psychology there. So I told these guys now—I said, "We'll just get the approaches to the hall, see." One of us coming along that corner, on across and so on, see. And you'd tell these guys to come along, that the union men were standing over on the sidewalk across from the hall. And they did. Jesus, none of them wanted to admit that he wasn't a union man then, now the chips is down, see. And so they come very hesitating—I would watch, you know, and I got a bang out of it—they'd kind of hesitate to the corner, then they'd turn left and go up the street and they'd come the other way and turn right. So pretty soon, they was dribbling over, dribbling over to the other side. And of course in about 15 to 20 minutes, why that looked pretty impressive to those coming along, straggling along a little bit later. Why hell, half the waterfront guys was over where the union men would be by that time, you know. And they're convinced. And so they go over there too. Just about—probably if it was that many—it wasn't more than ten gangs went to the hall that morning, and the rest of them were still watching to see if it would be safe to go across. Didn't have the nerve. So across the—they just probably kept them there all day long—they stayed there, and a lot of going on and so on. And the cops started coming around, and nothing happened. But the next day, however, it did. Next day the cops are down there in force led by—I forget what his name was, now—but he was an ex-general or colonel or some goddamn thing in the army with the State Police, you know. And he started getting rough, you know, pushing around, and so, hell, you couldn't let that go on, so I went to him, and I said, "Hey mister," I said, "You just got to cut this shit out." I said, "We got a right to be here, and you guys haven't, you know." I said, "We work here," and I said, "You just quit rattling that sword, because you're not scaring any-body. And he started getting tough with me, and I says, "All right, if you want it, you haven't got enough men here," I says, "to do any good for you." I says,

"Well, go ahead and—" Well, he decided he wouldn't get tough, so tough—and he just kept talking instead of, you know, trying to stir something up. Cops came along, and there was a few little mix-ups, but we had planned out pretty good that we would try to isolate the cops, you know—four or five guys around every goddamned one of them, you know. So they couldn't really organize and get together, and of course they never had the experience, you know, with crowds of our size. We must have had a thousand—not all our own people—a lot of unemployeds there. Matter of fact, at one time on the picket lines we had five thousand men on the Portland waterfront—did you know that? They're from these unemployed groups, you know.

In this way the strike began, with nominal control of the union in the hands of officials of the craft-union tradition, inexperienced and doubtful as to how to organize and direct such a venture. But actual control of the organization of the strike was in better and more experienced hands, those of the former Wobblies, who had participated in many kinds of strikes in many places. The actual conduct of the strike bears the unmistakable stamp of the IWW—physical violence and sabotage.

THE BATTLES

During the strike a number of battles took place between the union men and strike breakers and were of the utmost importance in welding the longshoremen into a real group rather than a mere agglomeration of people engaged in the same occupation. The strikers were organized into two action groups, picket squads and "riot" or "flying" squads. The picket squads were the men who did the actual picketing, and the "riot" squads performed military and police functions. Indeed, these "riot" squads actually policed the waterfront and kept order during most of the strike. This was not their only duty, however. Their chief task was to harrass actual or potential strikebreakers and to protect the picket squads from violence on the part of the employers' men. They were very successful at this. The only docks at which the employers were able to continue operations were at Terminal Number Four and the Luckenbach Dock where fences were erected and the docks became virtual fortresses. Terminal Four was in fact dubbed "Fort Carson" by the strikers.

One of the most famous battles fought during the 1934 strike was the raid on the McCormick Dock. After the onset of the strike, the waterfront employers hired a number of special police for the avowed intent of protecting their property and the nonstriking longshoremen. The longshoremen, on the other hand, alleged that these special police were in fact imported strong arm men, whose actual function was to intimidate the longshoremen. If this was their actual purpose, there is no indication that they enjoyed any degree of success. Because of the activities of the flying squads, the employers found it nearly impossible to move either strikebreakers or special police to and from the docks and so housed them either on the docks or aboard anchored ships.

The Admiral Evans was one of the ships devoted exclusively to housing special police. It was docked at the McCormick Dock under the Broadway bridge and the strikebreakers and special police were transported from the Admiral Evans to other docks in a motorboat. A high wooden fence had been erected in front of the dock to exclude the striking longshoremen. Eventually, however, the weakness of this fence compared with the steel and barbed wire fences surrounding the other barricaded docks came to the attention of the leader of the flying squads and a raid was organized.

The number of longshoremen involved in this raid cannot be determined but several longshoremen who participated have estimated the number at someplace between seventy-five and one hundred men. Several incidents took place during the raid that illustrate the sympathy the citizens of Portland felt toward the strikers. The wooden fence was assaulted by all of the longshoremen present and most of it collapsed inward. A number of nails were protruding from the boards. As the longshoremen clambered over the fence, a regular Portland policeman who had been guarding the gate is alleged to have admonished them to be careful not to step on the nails.

Once the strikers were inside the fence, the special police retreated aboard the Admiral Evans, pulled up the gang plank, and, arming themselves with clubs, prepared to repel the expected boarders. The rail of the ship stood about eight feet above the level of the dock which made it seem impossible for the longshoremen to gain access to it. While the majority of the raiders and union men congregated at one end of the ship, one longshoreman climbed aboard at the stern bearing the lower half of a sweeper's broom as a weapon, and assaulted the group of special police. While their attention was thus distracted, the remainder of the longshoremen swarmed onto the ship. Victory aboard the Admiral Evans was soon gained by the longshoremen.

The account of this raid as given above is built out of the accounts of several men, but the account given me by the leader of the assault on the Admiral Evans is as follows:

> There was a bunch of specials on the Evans, Admiral Evans. That was parked between McCormick and right under the Broadway Bridge there and Crown Mill, I guess it is. Had a big barricade across there. And that morning there was another bunch in the McCormick too. And I said, "We'll get that bunch that's in the McCormick. We'll get them out at three o'clock." At three o'clock we went down there and every boat in the city was there. So I says, "We can't do it." I says, "You guys, three or four of you at a time, just start whittling and walk up to the other end of the dock and we'll take the Admiral Evans." I says, "When I see enough men up there, I'll be up there." We were all down at this end whittling away, walking slow like nothing happened. Pretty soon I came by in the little old Ford I had and I see there was about fifty or seventy-five men there, and I says, "Let's go." They had a barricade there, and they helped me over the barricade and called to the special police that was on the dock. Soon as they seen us coming they went on the ship. Right after I got in, why they [the longshoremen] pulled the barricade down and here they came, see. The ship was up, oh, maybe about eight feet high, you know, and—amidship—and them guys [the specials on the ship] standing there with their clubs and everything. And we was talking to them down below. So I just snuck around to the other end, and I clumb onto the ship, and I got me an old broom. I came right down amidship and I just started wading into them guys with the broom. That drew their attention and here come everybody [the longshoremen] over

Bloody Thursday parade approaching the seawall. Note the prominence of the flags and the two longshoremen in uniform. (Photo by Oregon Journal*)*

the side. Some of those specials jumped in the river, got knocked in the river and everything else. That broke up their playhouse.

Each of these fights with strikebreakers and special police enhanced the growing feelings of group solidarity. Bitterness at the corrupt and unfair activities of the employers during the years since the 1922 strike found release in these battles. Many of these men had long suppressed the urge to strike a foreman or other employer representative, and the battles during the strike gave them their chance. Men who took part in these military activities still display apparent glee when talking about various phases of the campaign. The strike had for the longshoremen exactly the effect a "just" war does for a nation: it gave a great feeling of being engaged in important historical processes and working together toward a common cause. Differing personal goals and ambitions became irrelevant; it was the common cause that was important. This powerful feeling has lasted up to the present day although in much diminished form.

THE WARRIORS

There are many waterfront legends and myths centered around the 1934 strike and especially around the exploits of the men who formed the riot squads. Some of these men have become truly legendary figures and the tales of their exploits are told and retold, growing somewhat in the telling. Although all of the men who participated in the 1934 strike form a separate category among the long-shoremen (the '34 men), and stand as examples of appropriate union conduct for the younger men, the fighting men of the riot squads offer living testimonial to the fact that battles were fought and won. The legends of the group center around these heroic figures, and, indeed, a special deference is shown to these now griz-zled warriors. Although they have no official privileged status within the union, they are often excused for behavior that would bring heavy sanctions down upon any other member of the union. One of these men is now a notorious drunk, a

Memorial Stamp given to longshoremen who march in the Bloody Thursday parade.

condition with which the union grievance board is usually in little sympathy, and men who appear before this board charged with being drunk on the job or in the hiring hall are usually severely penalized. This individual, however, has been before the board on this charge many times, but no serious action has ever been taken against him, because, as one board member stated, "I couldn't forget what he did in '34." Any real penalty imposed on this man or his fellows would be analogous to a Philadelphia court sentencing John Paul Jones to jail for being drunk on the street. Often enough when he shows up on a job drunk, the other men simply do his work and let him sleep it off, or cover for him in some other way.

More important than this special status is the effect these men have on the attitudes of the younger men. The drunk mentioned above is the exception, not the rule. Many of these men drink, but very few are drunks. Their actions in 1934, arrogantly riding around in cars with thonged clubs hung on the sides to advertise their identity, and the reckless way in which many of them fought both strikebreakers and police, has elicited not only the admiration of the younger men, but also their envy. They too would like to make their names in this manner. The situation is reminiscent of that reported among the Sioux shortly after they were placed on reservations. The young men were rebellious and envious of the noted warriors. They too wanted to count coups and have the tales of their exploits told around the tribal fires. Consequently, many of the young men are openly contemptuous and insolent toward company representatives, and engaged in the 1971 strike (the first West Coast strike in 23 years) as though it were a vacation. They only regret that there are no strikebreakers and company goons for them to battle, since this means that they can engage in no heroic battles against the "forces of evil."

BLOODY THURSDAY

Much of the impact of these older heroes on the younger men would be lost were it not for the Bloody Thursday ritual. On July 5, 1934, an employer drive to reopen the Pacific Coast ports resulted in violent clashes between the police and union pickets in all of the major ports. Several longshoremen were killed in these clashes. The day on which they began was dubbed "Bloody Thursday" by the longshoremen, and large-scale memorial demonstrations for the men killed were held in all major West Coast ports. This memorial is still held up and down the Pacific Coast and all ports are still closed on this day. Although no one was killed in Portland, the largest and most impressive memorial is held there. This memorial consists of a two-mile parade and a memorial service held at the downtown seawall where navy ships are normally docked on more festive occasions. It is a point of honor for many of the veterans of the 1934 strike to attend this ritual, and it affords them an opportunity to visit with old friends and to meet or be seen by many of the younger longshoremen.

For the longshoremen the Bloody Thursday memorial serves the same function that Memorial Day once did for all Americans (Warner 1953), but it is of much greater significance to the longshoremen than Memorial Day. Bloody Thursday serves as a ritual to reaffirm group solidarity and group goals and ideals, the goals and ideals of the founders of the union. The memorial service held at the seawall always includes a benediction by some member of the clergy, usually one associated with union activism, and an exhortation by some distinguished member of the union not to forget the sacrifices and struggles of the men who formed the union. This always carries with it the implication, sometimes expressed and sometimes not, that the employers should not be forgiven their bloody-handed dealings with the union in its early days, as well as the implication that it could all happen again. Therefore, if the younger men are not prepared to fight as hard as their predecessors, a return to the miserable working conditions that prevailed before 1934 is more than possible.

SUBSEQUENT DEVELOPMENTS

The 1934 strike ended on July 31. There followed several months of negotiations and arbitration, but the outcome was a complete victory for the longshoremen's union. Although the hiring hall was designated as a joint union-employer hall, the union had practical control of the hiring process, a closed shop agreement, and the six-hour straight time day. The six-hour day, however, was not enforced for long. One of the advantages that had come to the longshoremen from the employers' regime was the *opportunity* to work a great deal of overtime when there was work available. Most of the longshoremen felt that the six-hour day at the straight time rate was insufficient, and longer work shifts soon were reinstated. It was many years before the standard work shift was reduced to the eight-hour day enforced by Local 6 before 1922.

Between 1934 and 1937, the Portland longshoremen were represented by Local 38-37 of the International Longshoremen's Association, but in 1937 the Portland longshoremen, along with most of the other longshoremen on the Pacific Coast, left the ILA and affiliated with the newly formed International Longshoremen's and Warehousemen's Union as Local 8. This switchover was an expression of the dislike for the leadership of the ILA, notably Joseph P. Ryan, and some of their own local officials, some of whom left the Portland waterfront permanently in 1937. This event marked the end of any semblance of the Portland Longshore Union to a craft union. The ILWU was affiliated with the Congress of Industrial Organizations and the ILA was affiliated with the American Federation of Labor. The men who left Local 8 in 1937 are commonly referred to as the "phonies" because of their close attachment to the AFL and the principles of craft unionism and the widely held belief that they were seeking to make "pie card" jobs for themselves as local or international officials.

5 / The union: present structure and hiring system

IDEOLOGICAL ORIGINS OF THE UNION

The ideological origins of the Portland Longshore Union are not to be found in the Communist party dogma, as has often been claimed, but rather in the basic concepts and principles of the Industrial Workers of the World and the American trade union movement. The features that have usually been thought to be communist derived or "inspired" are shared by both the communists and the IWW. One of the main concepts of the IWW was the overthrow of the capitalist system and its immediate replacement by a workers' democracy based on industrial divisions. The IWW, or Wobblies, called this process the "workers' revolution" and referred to every strike as a revolution. Unlike the Communists, the Wobblies did not believe in the violent overthrow of the government but advocated a form of civil disobedience. They believed that the revolution could only come about by organizing all of the workers in the country into "one big union" and then taking this union out on strike (the revolution). This would cause the collapse of the capitalist society, and the workers (Wobblies) would simply take over the existing industrial structure and operate it through workers' committees (Kornbluh 1964; Foner 1965; and Renshaw 1967). Another feature of Wobbly ideology inherited by the Portland longshoremen is the concept of "direct action" or sabotage, and the use of this tactic has again been mistaken for communist activity. The term is often understood to mean the destruction of productive machinery, but that is not the way it was generally used by the Wobblies. By sabotage or direct action they usually meant the "slowdown," but seldom the destruction of property.

The influence of the IWW appears in many other places and makes it quite apparent that these concepts and behavior were derived from the IWW and not from the Communists. On the second page of the Constitution of ILWU Local 8 (ILWU Local 8, 1960) appears the lone phrase:

OUR MOTTO
An Injury to One Is an Injury to All

This modified version of the original IWW motto was used by the IWW itself in 1913 (Kornbluh 1964). Many of the charter members of the ILA Local 38–78 (now ILWU Local 8) were ex-members of the IWW as has been noted above and their notable socialistic bias has often appeared in official statements issued by the union and expresses itself unmistakably in the hiring system. (See Hiring System below.) The organization and conduct of the 1934 strike with its harassment of strikebreakers and semi secret organization was also characteristic of the IWW. Confusion of Wobblies and communists was furthered by the Wobbly's proud boast that he carried a "red card," the term used for an IWW membership card.

Perhaps the most important and lasting concept inherited by the Portland Long-shore Union from the IWW is that of industrial unionism. Dissatisfaction with craft unionism was one of the forces that created the IWW, and the singular lack of success of the previous Portland longshore unions that had been organized along craft lines did not encourage the Portland longshoremen to emulate this model in 1934. The chief difference between craft and industrial unions is that a craft union only includes persons sharing some particular skill or who perform a special task, even though there may be many other persons working in the same plant or industry. An industrial union includes all of the workers in a plant or industry within its ranks or at least attempts to do so. In the past, craft unions had not been in the habit of respecting one another's picket lines and so one union (craft) might be striking in a plant while all of the other crafts might be working. This is clearly a weaker bargaining position than that enjoyed by an industrial union which would take all of the workers in the plant out on strike at the same time.

One of the features of the old craft unions and especially of the ILA to which the Portland longshoremen attributed the failure of former Portland longshore unions, and thus found extremely distasteful, was the "pie card" official (the union official whose effective tenure of office was for life). They believed, and still believe, that such officials spend too much of their time in obtaining personal financial gain and securing their tenure in office to care properly for the interests of the members of their unions. They believed that this tendency among permanent union officials leads them to "sell out" their followers, and the political structure and organization of the Portland Longshore Union was specifically designed to prevent this from happening to its officials.

POLITICAL STRUCTURES AND PROCESSES

The development of union oligarchy was prevented in Local 8 by the planning of the founders of the local. None of the factors that contribute to this state are accidental. The means used was the control of the accumulation of power in the hands of one man or a small group of men. The structure of the union and the nature of the political process within the Local were well designed to achieve this end through the following means:

1. No one is allowed to be an official of the Local who is not a full-time working longshoreman.
2. The tenure of office of all salaried officials is severely restricted and regu-lated, and all officers are subject to recall.
3. The nature of the rules of succession.
4. There is always a large pool of politically skilled men ready to step into any of the offices: there can be no appeal to their own superior experience

Longshoreman voting in local election. All but the man in striped overalls are pensioners who maintain an active role in the union by conducting the elections and counting ballots. (Photo by Gordon Clark)

by a small cadre of officials to support their candidacy for office against others because of the large number of local offices.

5. All major decisions by officials of the executive board must be confirmed by a membership meeting before they can be acted upon.

6. All members of the local are constrained to attend the meetings of the local and to vote in the elections.

The titled officers of Local 8 of the International Longshoremen's and Warehousemen's Union are the President, Vice-President, Financial Secretary-Treasurer, Marshal, two Business Agents, three Trustees, three Labor Relations Committeemen, and the Earnings Clerk. Only the Business Agents, Earnings Clerk, President, and Secretary-Treasurer are full-time paid officials. The dispatchers are quasi officials and for many purposes are treated as though they were officials, but they are actually joint employees of the union and employers. Tenure of office for all officials is one year. Salaried officials are not allowed to succeed themselves nor may they take any other salaried position in the union upon leaving a salaried position. The Constitution of the Local reads:

All salaried officials will not be allowed to succeed themselves or other salaried official positions unless they have not served a full term of one year upon time to vacate office (ILWU Local 8, 1960).

Other officials of the Local consist of the twenty-five members of the Executive Board and the twenty-one members of the Grievance Board. Elections for these offices are held once a year by secret ballot of the entire membership of the local. Primaries are held for all of the titled offices of the Local, and the two highest men for each office are again voted on in the final elections. The Executive and Grievance Boards are selected by plurality: the twenty-five and twenty-one highest scoring candidates for each board are those elected. All officials of the Local are subject to recall, a process that can be initiated by petition of 15% of the membership (ILWU Local 8, 1960).

The President is supposed to be the executive officer of the Local, but much of the day-to-day decision making process falls upon the Secretary-Treasurer. The Executive Board carries out the legislative functions necessary to the Local, but all of their decisions must come before the full membership meeting in the form of Executive Board recommendations and must be ratified by the membership before they are entered into the rules of the Local. In other words, the Executive Board is the deliberative and law formulating body, but none of the "laws" they enact can become binding until ratified by a membership meeting in which at least 300 of the members are present. This is not a rubber-stamp procedure. Small issues are often voted on and passed without much argument, but matters of importance to the membership are not only argued on the floor of the membership meetings as much as they are in the Executive Board. The Executive Board recommendations are often much modified by the membership or simply voted down and discarded.

The final decision in all of the affairs of the Local must be made by the membership in regular stop-work meetings held on the second Wednesday of each month. The membership is extremely active in attending meetings and turning out for elections. One of the reasons for this is that all members are fined for nonattendance of meetings and for not voting in elections. Missing one meeting or failing to vote once does not entail a serious fine, but missing three meetings in succession entails a heavy fine and an appearance before the Grievance Board as does the consistent failure to vote.

The Grievance Board is one of the unique features of the ILWU. The membership is disciplined for small and some not-so-small transgressions on the job by the Grievance Board. Discipline is not usually left to the employer, and the union disapproves of men being sent to the Joint Labor Relations Committee for disciplinary action. This board also handles all violations of union rules by members of the Local. The process followed is not always a model of the best jurisprudence, but it is unusually effective. The penalties handed down by the Board for what, for example, appears on the books as a first violation drunk charge may often seem excessive; but in many cases the members of the Board know that the man is a habitual drunk and that he is making his first appearance before the Board only because he has never been cited before. The Board is analogous to a family sitting in judgment on one of its members, because the board members are all working longshoremen and may often work with the offender and know him quite well, and their decision is based to a great extent on personal knowledge of the defendant. The Board's decision is not final unless the defendant has pleaded "guilty" to the charges. If he enters a plea of "not guilty" he may appeal the Board's decision if he thinks it excessive or unfair. This procedure is not often used capriciously, because it has long been customary for some member to move to double the penalty if the appellant is patently guilty and has not been treated unfairly by the Grievance Board. False accusation has customarily been dealt with by "reversing the charges" and convicting the accuser of the charge placed against the original defendant.

There is at all times a large pool of politically skilled longshoremen available for the various offices of the Local. Out of a total membership of about 920, fifty-six men are officials of the Local at any given time. Of these, seven, including the dispatchers, are full-time salaried officials, and none of them may occupy office more than a year nor seek another salaried office. Hence, their tenure is only one year and the annual turnover of all officials, salaried or otherwise, is great. There are no figures available as to how many men not in office at present have held some office at one time or another, but an estimate of about three men for every official position does not seem excessive, and this is probably a much too conservative estimate. This means that somewhere around a fourth of the Portland longshoremen have held some kind of political office in the local.

FACTIONS

Until fairly recently, Local 8 had three active political factions. One was composed of left-wing radicals (originally the IWW group and other persons of left-wing inclinations); a second group was formed of Catholic trade unionists of one kind or another; and the third was a right-wing faction. These groups were very active, well organized, and influential up to and through the decade of the 1950s, and major decisions of the Local were very often influenced by the alignments of these three factions. Generally, the left wing could be expected to support the actions of the International and Harry Bridges, and the others could be expected to oppose them. The left wing was the largest and most influential faction throughout the history of the Local and usually dominated the other factions to a great degree because they were usually at odds with one another. This was not always true when the interests of the Catholics and the right wing coincided as they sometimes did, especially in opposition to Bridges' efforts to integrate Local 8. This task was finally accomplished through a coalition of the left wing and the Catholics after the Catholic church took an integrationist position.

The last factionalist development, in the 1960s, brought an end to the traditional three factions. As the composition of the membership shifted away from older men who had been charter members of the Local ('34 men) and toward younger men (Johnny-come-latelies) who had come to the waterfront in the late 1940s and 1950s, these factions began to decline. Partially this is because many of the older men had retired and left the Local, and among these older men were the most skillful of the local politicians. More and more younger men ran for and were elected to office and the younger men would often vote for one man and against another simply because he was a member of his age group. When the union membership had shifted to the extent that the younger men formed a majority, it became less and less likely that an older man would be elected to office if he ran against one of the younger men. These two factors, the retirement of many of the older skilled politicians belonging to one of the three traditional factions, and the appearance of new factional lines based on age, destroyed the influence of the former factions. The new factions were simply those of the older men and the younger men. This is a difficult form of factionalism to maintain because of the difficulty of deciding who is in which faction: there was no clear dividing line after the " '34 men" retired. The younger men had completely taken over the Local by 1967 and there were no discernible organized factions left within the Local.

Only the left-wing faction has had a lasting impact on the attitudes of the younger men. The IWW tradition is still carried on by the young longshoremen. Men may often be heard to repeat Wobbly slogans who have only a vague idea of what the IWW was and do not know that these utterances originated with the IWW. One of these concepts most often given voice is the opinion that racial discrimination is a plot of the employers which has the sole purpose of dividing and oppressing working men. This has had important implications in reference to the stand toward integration taken by the local. (See Race Relations below.)

THE HIRING SYSTEM

To the Portland longshoremen the hiring system used to dispatch longshoremen, to their jobs in Portland is a great deal more than that. The hiring system and hiring hall lie at the very heart of the longshoreman's way of life. The inordinate fondness of these men for their hiring system has been expressed very convincingly by their resistance to every attempt to change that system by the employers or the International Union. In the 1948 strike, which was the result of an employer attempt to regain control of the hiring hall, the Portland longshoremen displayed the solidarity of their opinion by a total boycott of the NLRB "final offer" election. Not one longshoremen voted. Again, in 1966 during contract negotiations when it was proposed that other methods of dispatching be tried on an experimental basis in the major ports, the Portland delegation had the Port of Portland declared not a major port for such purposes (ILWU 1966). The system as originally designed has undergone some changes since 1934; however, these changes were all initiated within the Local itself. Some of the changes were inspired by outside influences such as the Taft–Hartley Act, but the Local itself decided how to implement such changes as would allow them to comply with the law. No really basic changes, changes that might be seen as contradictory to the original intent to distribute the work fairly among all of the regular longshore work force, have been made. The basis of the hiring system established in 1934 is still intact.

RECRUITMENT

The procedures for selecting new longshoremen—that is, for screening applicants and deciding which ones are acceptable—have been formally adopted by the union and comply with the appropriate legal requirements (ILWU 1952). The first step is a move by either the employer or the union in a joint Labor Relations Committee meeting to put on more permits or B men. If this is agreed to, the recommendation is taken to a membership meeting of the union and voted on there, and advertisements are placed in the local newspapers stating that applications are being taken for longshoremen. The applications are screened by the employer and union committees, and the men who are qualified are given union permits and limited registration. This appears to be standard recruiting procedure for any organization seeking to employ a fairly large number of men. However, there are and have always been a number of informal procedures followed in recruiting longshoremen that are of more interest than the formal methods.

Throughout the history of the Portland waterfront the predominant method of recruitment has been the "brother-in-law" system. When new longshoremen were needed it was the usual practice for regular longshoremen to bring their friends and relatives to the attention of the appropriate authorities and they were always the first to be selected as potential regular longshoremen. There have been times when it was not absolutely necessary to be a friend or relative of a longshoreman to become a longshoreman or a member of the longshoremen's union, but it has nearly always been helpful.

The brother-in-law system employed by the previous longshoremen's union (ILA, Local 6) was destroyed by the members of the Waterfront Employers' Union in 1922, but they immediately replaced it with a similar system of their own. The present Portland longshore union has always been opposed to the brother-in-law system as a matter of policy, but in fact the system was used from the very inception of the local. Until World War II, it was very unlikely that any man who was not related to or a close friend of a longshoreman would have had any chance of becoming a regular longshoreman in Portland. At one time a whole series of union permits were issued to a group of men who are still collectively referred to as the "longshoremen's sons." These men were given permits and allowed to work on the waterfront solely because they were related to longshoremen.

During and after World War II, this system became steadily weaker, in part because there were few longshoremen's sons that were not in the armed forces during the war and because of the vastly increased need for longshoremen to handle the immense amount of war material that was being shipped out of Portland. The demand was high, not only because of the material being shipped to American forces in the Pacific, but to a great degree because of the terrific amount of cargo shipped from Portland to the Soviet Union via Vladivostok. A special dock and heavy lift crane were even erected in Portland to load locomotives and other railroad rolling stock onto Russian ships, many of which were built in Portland and Vancouver, Washington.

This wartime boom brought a greater demand for longshoremen than had existed since World War I. Many of the younger longshoremen were in the armed forces as were many of the relatives of the longshoremen, and for this reason other men, not related to longshoremen, had to be brought into the industry. The first significant group of outsiders since before 1934 came to the waterfront during this period and soon became known as the "war babies." The union could, of course, have avoided putting these men on as regular longshoremen, but this would have been contrary to the ideology inherited from the IWW. It did not want to have a large group of nonunion longshoremen working regularly in the port as had the earlier Portland longshore union. The Local's actions were also conditioned by the realization that having such a large group of nonunion men working in Portland would much weaken their collective bargaining position when the war ended. It might seem that the "war babies" would have helped to bring an end to the brother-in-law system, but rather than oppose the system, they were soon seeking to gain employment privileges for their friends and relatives. They accepted and used the same exclusivist system that would have barred them from the waterfront before World War II. The brother-in-law system was, however, damaged by the admission of so many outsiders to the longshore group and it never quite regained its former strength. It was further damaged by the Taft–Hartley Act, state and federal fair-employment laws, and most of all by the insistence of the International that the Portland Local admit Negroes to its ranks. The integration issue forced the union not only to accept Negroes, but to establish procedures for recruitment that are harder to circumvent or influence than were the older procedures.

The former procedure for starting out as a longshoreman was simple and informal, and it was here that the brother-in-law system operated. A man who wished to become a longshoreman needed only to be present in the hiring halls on days of peak activity when the supply of regular longshoremen was exhausted. The paymaster would then issue casual payroll cards to the number of men required to fill the day's needs. These casual men, or "white cards" as they were called because the payroll card they used was white as compared to a union permit man's yellow card, could continue to hang around the hiring hall and pick up overflow work on peak days as long as they performed satisfactorily on the job. It was not always necessary for a longshoreman's friend or kinsman to wait until the supply of men already holding casual cards was exhausted before obtaining one for himself.

My own case is a good illustration of the differential treatment of longshore kin. When I started on the waterfront, my father took me into the hiring hall and introduced me to the dispatchers. I was then instructed that I would have to wait for a day when the entire labor force was employed and that I had best remain in the hall during all hiring periods until that time. I spent about four fruitless days waiting for an opportunity, but during this time there were always white cards that had not been dispatched. On the fifth morning, the dispatcher who was an old friend of my father hid a job slip until the hiring period was completed. He had previously instructed me not to leave the hall after the hiring period as the other men would, so that I would be available immediately afterwards. When the hall was empty of other men seeking white cards and longshoremen, I was issued a payroll card and sent to my first longshore job. The dispatcher would not have considered violating the standard procedures for obtaining a casual card for anyone who was not a kinsman or close friend of another longshoreman. I was never again shown any favoritism by anyone in the union, nor to my knowledge was anyone else. The other stages of status advancement were closely observed and regulated, and no abrogation of the procedures was permitted.

The casual men holding white cards were, however, given a certain preference for obtaining union permits on the basis that they were experienced men who had worked in the industry and had already demonstrated their competence and ambition. Among men who had not worked on the waterfront before obtaining union permits, longshoremen's relatives were a preferred category. The union was later forced to abandon these practices because it was thought to afford too much opportunity for racial discrimination, and new procedures were adopted that eliminated discrimination and preferential recruiting.

STATUS CATEGORIES

After the 1934 strike was settled the union and employers established a list of "registered" longshoremen. These men were to constitute the regular work force, and were to be dispatched before anyone else. The primary criterion for deciding who should or should not be on the registration list was seniority—time in the industry. Men who were of doubtful status or who had not worked steadily enough before the strike were designated "permit men." From the very beginning the union has exerted every effort to equate registration with union membership. The original list of registered men were all union members, and the union wanted very much to retain this relationship in order to avoid the problems that ILA Local 6 had in 1922. Men who were not on the registration list but had worked on the waterfront and aspired to become regular longshoremen were given union permits. The first status categories, then, were those of union members and union permits.

After the passage of the Taft–Hartley Act, this was untenable, because the preferred hiring of union members became illegal under certain provisions of the National Labor Relations Act (Cox and Bok 1962). The language of the agreement between the union and employers had to be changed, and although the original categories were retained, their labels were transformed. The first alteration was to designate the previous category of union members fully registered longshoremen, and the "permit men" limited registration longshoremen. A third category had existed from the inception of union control of hiring in 1934 and had been variously called casuals or "white cards." This category of men had always had a certain informal status and had been the pool from which new permit men were chosen, but the thirty-day provisions of the NLRA made this impractical after the insertion of Section 8 (b) from the Labor–Management Relations Act (Cox and Bok 1962) which provided that unfair labor practices charges might be brought against unions. The "white cards" had to be stripped of any legal standing in the longshore industry in order for the union to continue to have an effective collective bargaining position, because, under the older procedures, all any man needed to do to become a registered longshoreman would be to work on the waterfront for thirty days as a casual and then demand union membership and registration. This would have produced a situation where there were so many registered longshoremen in the port that none of them could make a living on the waterfront. The Pedro Formula (ILWU 1952) was the answer to this problem. The three new categories were:

1. Registered longshoremen.   (A)
2. Limited registration longshoremen.   (B)
3. Casual men. (No status as longshoremen.)   (Y)

The designation of these categories, A, B, and Y came later.

The registered longshoremen (A men) together with the limited registration longshoremen (B men) constitute the regular work force. The A men hold the top status and have permanent tenure as longshoremen barring serious misdemeanors. The B men do not have permanent tenure and may be removed from the registration list (which effectively means from the industry) by the Joint Labor Relations Committee for reasons that would not even bring a reprimand to an A man (ILWU 1952). As indicated above, Y men have no standing in the industry. The practice of recruiting new B men from the Y category was, however, retained long after it was formally abolished, and it is from this practice that much of the Local's resistance to the proposals of the International dealing with integration originated. Over the years, this informal procedure had become so firmly entrenched that the longshoremen saw the progression from Y to B status as the only legitimate procedure, just as the progression from B to A status is the only legitimate way to become an A man. Any person wishing to become a longshoreman had only to come to the hiring hall on a peak day, wait until all of the A, B, and Y men had either been hired or determined not to work on that day, and if there was still a need for longshoremen, he would be given a Y card and sent to a job. When the ILWU and PMA (Pacific Maritime Association) jointly advertised for additional B men, he could then apply for B status. At this point anyone could apply for B status also, but the Y man was given credit for experience in the industry. As can readily be seen, this meant that the Y man retained his previous advantage over men who had not worked on the waterfront.

The International's objection to this finally prevailed and the system had to be abandoned. The manner in which this took place is revealing in regard to the way the Portland longshoremen see their hiring process and of the emotional load connected with the hiring hall and the traditional hiring and recruiting procedures. The Portland Local had long been at odds with the officials of the International and with some other locals over its refusal to admit Negroes to its ranks, thus effectively barring them from the industry. Prior to 1961, no Negroes had been allowed to work in the port in any category, with the exception of one man in the 1940s and a few visitors from other ports who had been allowed to work in Portland for short periods. This was partially due to the low number of Negroes residing in the Portland area before World War II, but racial prejudice had played an important part.

In 1960, the union negotiated a new contract as a part of which the port registration lists were consolidated into a coast-wide registration list. The import of this is that the International now handled the process of placing men on the registration list and not the locals. Most of the processing was still handled at the local level and the locals made their own decisions concerning whether or not to take an individual into the union, but the final step of moving to place a man officially on the registration list was in the hands of the International. This gave the International the lever it had long sought. Local 8 had about 100 men on the B list at the time that this contract was negotiated, and the International simply refused to move to place these men on the A list until the Local allowed Negroes to work in their port. As had always been the case, many of these B men were either the close kin or friends of A men, who were understandably interested in seeing to it that they were promoted to the A list. In 1961, Local 8 finally allowed Negroes to work as casual men, the first step in the traditional recruitment procedure, and many of the members of the local, including a number of officials, saw this as the first, and necessarily the first, step in the process of integrating the union. The International was, however, not satisfied with this action, insisting that the port was not integrated until there were Negroes on the A list, and steadfastly refused to place the Local 8 B men on the A list. The Local countered by taking all of the B men into the union and giving them the same work privileges as A men, thus circumventing the efforts of the International.

In the spring of 1963, Local 8 decided that it needed more men and moved to add one hundred men to the B list. This would have included all of the Y men who met the requirements for age and physical condition, including about ten Negroes. The International Union objected that this was not enough Negroes to begin to compensate for the years that Local 8 had refused to allow Negroes to work in the port, and flatly refused to allow any men to be placed on the B list, unless they were taken on a first-come, first-served basis, regardless of race. This would have meant violating a long standing tradition. Men had long attained A status in Local 8 in the same manner: first they were Y men, then B men, then A men. Some men had become B men without going through the Y stage simply because there were sometimes not enough Y men to fill all of the openings for B men, but Y men were usually, although unofficially, given preference for B status under these circumstances. The entire ILWU and not merely Local 8 had been extremely concerned with avoiding the problems of corruption and unfair hiring practices that had prevailed before 1934. One way of doing this was to institute regular procedures for recruitment into the industry and in daily hiring. It was inevitable that some of these would be institutionalized informal procedures, and it was also inevitable that these informal procedures would become emotionally important to the members of the Local.

The informal procedure of recruiting B men from the Y list served several functions. First, it assured that the new B men were committed to becoming longshoremen. Second, it gave the membership committee some basis on which to judge the prospective B men. Work reports submitted by gang bosses and other A men were available to the committee; the longshoremen on the committee may have actually worked with the candidates, and under such circumstances, they were often able to make personal evaluations. Third, and perhaps most important, having worked as a Y man gave the new B man, and eventual A man, a clear legitimacy in the eyes of his peers. That is to say, he had not received his status because he was someone's brother or son, or because he had greased anyone's palm. He had received his status because he had demonstrated to the satisfaction of his fellow workers that he was a willing and able worker. This procedure had no relation to the fact that for many years Negroes had not been admitted to the Local. Negroes had been turned away at the dispatch window, and would have been turned down in the course of any other procedure as well.

Over the years the older, more prejudiced men had left the waterfront through death or retirement, and the political structure of Local 8 had been taken over by the younger men. Most of the young people in the country are undoubtedly less prejudiced than their elders, and the Portland longshoremen are no exception to this. The older men who had previously been dispatchers had turned Negroes away either because they themselves were prejudiced or because they feared that a prejudiced membership would retaliate against them. The younger men were neither prejudiced nor did they believe the majority of the membership to be so.

To counter the International's "first-come, first-served" proposal, Local 8 proposed to place all of the Negro Y men on the B list, regardless of their qualifications or lack of qualifications, if Local 8 were to be allowed to process the remaining Y men in its customary fashion before considering anyone else for the B list. Some of the Negro Y men were not qualified for B status because of their age and physical condition; two of them were over the maximum age of forty. The International rejected this, claiming that it was a subterfuge to restrict the number of Negroes on the B list and insisted that its original proposal was the only one that they would consider. Local 8 continued to balk, and claimed that it was attempting no subterfuge but only attempting to protect men who they believed had established a right to first consideration for B status. At this point, the International sent the international Secretary-Treasurer to observe the situation and see if this impasse could be broken. He soon saw that the Local was quite sincere in insisting that it would take no other men unless the Y men were given first consideration. He then advanced the proposition that the Local be allowed to process the current Y men and place as many of them on the B list as it saw fit, but all Negroes on the list must be given B status regardless of age or other qualifications, and that an additional 200 men be placed on the B list on the "first come, first served" basis originally proposed by the International Union.

I was present at the next regular meeting and this proposal was heatedly discussed, but it was soon apparent that the only serious opposition was centered around the position of a few Y men who were members' sons and were not yet 21 and thus not admissible to B status. During the course of the meeting, the international officials agreed to waive the age requirements for these men, since it had already been waived for the over-age Negroes. Nearly the entire membership of the Local was present at the meeting, and when the vote was taken, it was overwhelmingly in favor of the Secretary-Treasurer's proposal.

THE HIRING HALL

As the hiring system is the very heart of the longshoremen's way of life, the hiring hall is the core of the hiring system, for it is here that all of the ideologies of the union men and the values of all of the longshoremen are clearly expressed. The location of the hall has changed over the years, but it is now located at NW 17th and Glisan Streets. The building is a converted church which presents quite a contrast to the red-light district location of some of the older halls. The hiring takes place twice a day. The day shift is dispatched from the hall at 7:00 a.m. and the night shifts are dispatched at 5:00 p.m. The procedures at both dispatch periods are identical, so I will describe only the day shift dispatching.

The longshoremen are dispatched in two manners. There are gang men and board men (hall men). The gangs are dispatched on a strict yearly earnings basis on the principle of low gang out first. The gang with the lowest earnings is dispatched first and to the longest job. The gang with the highest earnings is dispatched last and to the shortest job. The board men are also supposed to be dispatched by earnings, but in fact they are dispatched by rotation. Each A man has a plastic dowel (plug) with his registration number engraved into it. On any day when there are no plugs left in the boards, at fifteen minutes before seven, all of the men who wish to work place their plugs in padlocked boxes placed on shelves in front of the hiring boards. At seven o'clock, the dispatcher comes out of the dispatch office, picks up a box, and shakes it vigorously in several directions to assure that the plugs are well mixed. He then unlocks the box and starts removing the plugs at random and placing them in the board (a vertical piece of plywood with holes drilled in it to accommodate the plugs) starting at the upper right-hand corner and proceeding toward the left-hand side of the board. When the left-hand side is reached, he begins placing plugs in the next row of holes and so on until all of the plugs are placed in the board. (See Figure 4.) The hiring starts as the dispatcher removes the plugs from the board in the order in which they were inserted and calls the numbers engraved on the plugs. As each man answers his number and comes to the window, he picks what he thinks is the best job among those available. The longshoremen refer to this hiring procedure as a "Chinese lottery" and are extremely fond of it.

←								
8	7	6	5	4	3	2	1	1
16	15	14	13	12	11	10	9	2
24	23	22	21	20	19	18	17	3
32	31	30	29	28	27	26	25	4
40	39	38	37	36	35	34	33	5
48	47	46	45	44	43	42	41	6
56	55	54	53	52	51	50	49	7
64	63	62	61	60	59	58	57	8

FIGURE 4   Schematic diagram of hiring board showing order of hiring. The position of any one plug is determined solely by chance.

There are several hiring boards: the day ship board, the night ship board, the day dock board, the day lift board, the night lift board, day "old man's" board, and a night "old man's" board. Any class A registered longshoreman may "plug in" any of the boards at will, except the "old man's" and the lift boards. Only men who are qualified and registered as fork lift drivers may "plug in" the lift boards, and the "old man's" board is reserved for men over sixty years of age or who have been disabled so that they cannot perform the heavy labor hired on the dock and ship boards. Winch operators are hired directly out of the ship boards. Confusion between qualified winch operators and the other longshoremen is avoided by giving the winch operators black plugs and the other men white plugs.

If a man whose number has been called comes to the dispatch window and does not see a job he wants, he has the option of refusing the work ("burning" his plug). He cannot leave his plug in the board if there is work available. Plugs left over (not called) are left in the board and are the first called for the next day's hiring. The next day the dispatcher starts putting the new plugs in behind those left over from the day before. At the end of the month all plugs are removed from the board and the process starts over again.

The dispatchers are restrained from displaying favoritism by the presence of the men whose plugs are being placed in the boards, standing around observing and frequently crowding the dispatcher. If any irregularity were observed, there are plenty of voices to call it to the dispatcher's attention. If he were suspected of purposely placing someone's plug in a favorable position by any method other than pure chance the odds are that a small riot would ensue, and the dispatcher would most certainly be discharged from his job and removed from the waterfront. The contract reads:

> 8.44 Any longshoreman or dispatching hall employee found guilty by the Joint Port Labor Relations Committee of favoritism or discrimination or bribery shall immediately be discharged and dropped from the registered list (ILWU–PMA 1966).

All regular longshoremen are very familar with this contract provision.

Class A registered longshoremen are required to work one day per month in order to maintain their status. Any of these men may refuse a job at any time with no penalty, and if already on a job may call the hall for a replacement. The only restriction is that if a longshoreman calls a replacement, he must take a full day off. He is not allowed to work for the next 24 hours.

B and Y men are hired by straight rotation with no pretense of being dispatched by earnings. Like the A men, B men have plugs and a hiring board (separate from those of the A men) in which their plugs are placed at the hiring periods. They are hired after the A men and before the Y men, but have no option to choose their jobs and may not refuse a work opportunity without penalty. Y men are the last hired and may not choose their jobs, and if they refuse work may be summarily sent from the hiring hall and from the waterfront. The basis of the hiring system is supposed to be complete equality in work opportunity for all longshoremen, but this equality only exists within the status categories. The B men are very much second-class citizens within the hiring hall context, since they do not share equal work opportunity with the A men. Their position is in many ways analogous to that of an apprentice, but although they do not have the powerful claim to tenure or job security enjoyed by the A men, they do have strong claims to job security and cannot be summarily dismissed from the waterfront as the Y men can. If the B men are second-class citizens, the Y men are much further from first-class status, which is reflected by the letter assigned to their category.

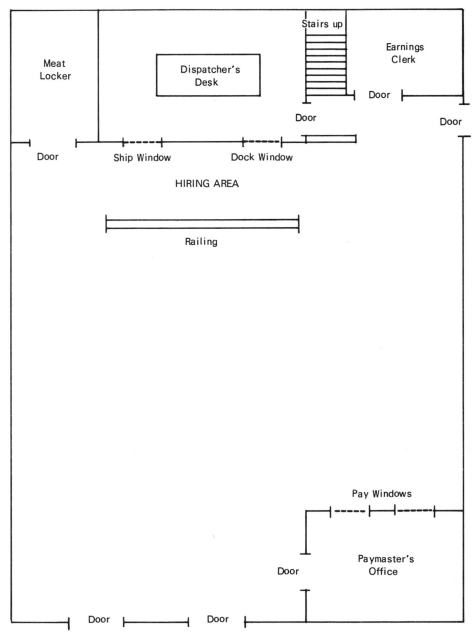

FIGURE 5 Schematic floor plan of the hiring hall.

APPRENTICESHIP AND OATH

B men are in many ways analogous to apprentices. They must work for two to four years in the B category, and their fitness to be advanced to A status is more than influenced by the A men. The behavior of B men both in the hall and on the job is determined to a great extent by the knowledge that the final judgment as to whether they will be promoted to A status will be made in a full membership meeting by the A men. Friends that they have made and also enemies will be in the meeting, and it is the membership who makes the final decision. The pressure to act in a manner appropriate to a longshoreman as seen by the A men is as ever-present as it is subtle. A B man is seldom told that his behavior is inappropriate except in regard to work performance, but there are a whole series of attitudes and behaviors that he must adopt if his prospective peers are not to be prejudiced against him. Among these are the simple matters of dressing properly, stance and posture, and engaging in the ritual of joking behavior in an appropriate manner.

After a B man has the approval of the Executive Board and Membership Committee and is recommended to the membership for acceptance into the union, he must come before a stop-work meeting and be passed on by the membership. Stop-work meetings are held on the second Wednesday of each month when all work on the waterfront is halted for the night. Usually about half of the membership is in attendance, and what is for them the usually humorous matter of voting on the prospective members is a tense and fearful performance for the candidates. The new men are simply lined up in the front of the hall and the President asks if there are any objections. If there are none, and there rarely are, the B men are sent from the room, and the vote is put to the membership.

If they are all accepted, as they normally are, they are called back in to take the oath, to be sworn into the union. The oath is as follows:

> I do most solemnly on my honor promise that during my connection with this Union I will remain a true and faithful member, observe its laws and labor as far as lies within my power to further the advancement of my trade, so that my fellow-men can receive and enjoy with me the just fruits of their labor. That I will attend the meetings of this Union as often as it is possible for me to do so; that I will not reveal, unless by permission, any of the secret workings that may at any time be confided to me; and I do further promise to assist a member of this Union when and wherever I may find him in distress; that I will never knowingly wrong him or his but will help preserve the rights of his household inviolate; and finally I will strive to create a brotherly feeling between our Union and organizations who mean to uphold the dignity of labor and to affirm the nobility of all who earn their bread by the sweat of their brow; that I will not deal in any manner with any person who is an enemy of labor. To this I pledge my honor (ILWU, Local 8 1960).

This is really a professional oath, demanding from the person taking it that he promise to conform not only in matters pertaining to his work and union in a manner appropriate to a union member but also in personal matters to the standards of the group. He promises to help another member when and where he "may find him in distress" and also that he will not violate the rights of his household. In no place is there any mention of the deity. The man swears solely on his honor and clearly is expected to be an honorable person. The violation of this oath is not a matter that is taken lightly by the members of Local 8. Once the oath is taken, a man is expected to be a full member of the group and to tailor his behavior to its norms. He is fully committed to the group.

6 / Race relations

Like most predominantly Caucasian occupational groups, until very recently, the Portland Longshore Union has not accepted Negro members or allowed Negroes to work within their jurisdiction. Unlike many others, however, there has not been a long history of powerful anti-Negro feeling and racial strife. It has been only since World War II that the question of whether or not Negroes should be admitted to the waterfront has become an issue on the Portland waterfront. This is not surprising because it is only since that time that the question of equal rights for minority groups has gained momentum within the United States. Previously, there was little question as to whether Negroes and members of other racial minorities should be excluded from membership in most unions, occupations, universities, fraternal organizations, and residential areas. They were simply excluded almost everywhere on the basis that they were inferior and undesirable. The state of Oregon, the city of Portland, and the Portland Longshore Union have not deviated widely from the national trend. However, the city and state have been somewhat more progressive than most in that the public schools were integrated in the late 1930s and the restaurants and public facilities in the mid-forties. The Portland Longshore Union did not, however, begin the process of integrating its ranks until 1961. This presents something of a problem, because the longshoremen in many ways represent a fair cross-section of the population of the state and their attitudes toward Negroes do not differ widely from those of most Oregonians.

Moreover, there are certain other aspects of Portland waterfront race relations that seem problematical. In the majority of contexts where Negroes have been excluded on the basis of bigotry or racial prejudice, they have not been the only racial or ethnic group discriminated against. American Indians, Spanish Americans, Orientals and other nonwhite groups have also been subject to much the same restrictions as have Negroes. Usually, this exclusion has reached further than race and has resulted in discrimination against religious and national groups. The strongholds of racial discrimination have also been strongholds of anti-Semitism, anti-Catholicism, and xenophobia. But this complex has never existed in the Portland longshore group or the union. Indians, Mexicans, Jews, Catholics, and aliens have never been barred from waterfront employment or membership in the union. To the contrary, representatives of all of these categories have always been members of the group. This is not to deny that some longshoremen are prejudiced against these groups of people, but such prejudice has never been sufficiently widespread to precipitate discriminatory action, and derogatory comments about these persons are extremely rare except in the context of the ceremonially licensed joking behavior, which in itself signifies total acceptance of the person toward whom it is directed. (See Joking Behavior, page 102.)

Thus, it seems clear that simple racial prejudice, if such a complex set of notions, attitudes, and emotions may be called simple, is not the only or even the main factor in the exclusion of Negroes from the Portland waterfront and the longshore union, and according to my older informants, it has never been a matter of great concern to most of the Portland longshoremen. Nonetheless, the fact stands that Negroes were not allowed to work on the Portland waterfront until 1961, and there is at present a certain amount of anti-Negro feeling among the longshoremen.

There are several reasons for this situation: the history of the city; the size of the Negro community; the political structure of the union; the ideology of the union; various forms of status rivalry between Negroes and whites and among the Negroes themselves; perceived violations of the symbolic behavior system of the white longshoremen; and most important, the challenge presented by the International Union and civil rights groups to the traditional methods of attaining union membership, and, thus, to the legitimate acquisition of the status of a longshoreman in the eyes of the other longshoremen.

HISTORICAL FACTORS

One of the most important of the factors that helped establish the tradition of Negro exclusion from the Portland waterfront is the tiny size of the Negro community. As late as 1940, there were only 2,565 Negroes in the state and although the vast majority resided in the Portland Metropolitan Area, Negroes (2,040) comprised only 0.6% of the population of Portland. It was possible to live in Portland prior to 1941 and be unaware of the existence of Negroes in the city. There were almost as many longshoremen in the port as there were Negroes in the city, and many of the employable male Negroes were holding jobs with the railroads. By 1960, the number of Negroes in the Portland area had increased to 16,429, an eight-fold increase, but they still only constituted 2.1% of the population of the urban area.

The size of the Negro community did not make it an attractive source of labor for the shipping industry or even a source of strikebreakers during labor disputes, since it could not have supplied enough unemployed and physically fit males to meet the demands of the longshore industry at any time in its history. The effects of this were double. There was no incentive for the waterfront employers to recruit Negro labor and in fact they refused to employ any Negroes, as is evidenced by a form letter answering a prospective longshoreman's application for employment: ". . . we employ white labor only" (WEU May 8, 1922). This letter was dispatched during the 1922 longshore strike when the Waterfront Employers' Union was recruiting strikebreakers. This policy on the part of the employers firmly established the tradition of Negro exclusion from the longshore union, for there were no Negro longshoremen working in the port when the union was first organized, hence the union began as a completely non-Negro organization, and partially due to the depression recruited very few new members for a number of years. On the other hand, anti-Negro feelings among the Portland longshoremen had not been exacerbated by the use of Negro strikebreakers, as has happened in so many other cases. But the anti-Negro stance of the Waterfront Employers' Union made the Portland waterfront a congenial place for persons of extreme right-wing convictions, a circumstance that helped to setback the cause of integration for almost twenty years.

The depression contributed to the exclusion of Negroes for the first ten years of the existence of the present longshoremen's union. The first registration rolls included only those men who had worked as longshoremen for one year before the 1934 strike and, as explained above, there were no Negroes among the longshoremen. Even at the beginning of World War II, when there was a great influx of Negroes into the area, no Negroes or any other new men were added to the rolls of the longshoremen's union, for the waterfront was so depressed through 1942 that many of the regular longshoremen left the waterfront and took jobs in the booming shipyards in order to make a living. Thus, there was no opportunity for Negroes to obtain employment as longshoremen until 1943. Even then, few outsiders came to the waterfront, because longshore wages lagged considerably behind those of other local industries until 1946, due to the union having accepted a wage freeze and a no-strike agreement for the duration of the war.

Another factor that militated against the inclusion of Negroes in the waterfront work force was the tendency toward nepotism, the "brother-in-law" system of recruitment inherited from the period before the formation of the present union. Although the founders of ILWU Local 8 had struggled against this practice from the very beginning, it was never completely extinguished, as it has never been altogether excised from any other group. Clearly, the selection for membership of only the relatives of white longshoremen would not admit black men to the union.

INTERNAL POLITICAL FACTORS

The left-wing radical faction of the union was strongly committed to the cause of integration and racial equality from the inception of the longshore union. It was, however, only one of three major factions within the union (see Chapter 5), and it was powerfully opposed by the smaller but extremely militant right wing and impeded by the disinterest of the majority of longshoremen in attaining these ends.

Nonetheless, the left-wing radicals were responsible for the first attempt to integrate the Portland Longshore Union. This had long been one of the goals of Harry Bridges and the entire left wing of the ILWU, because Portland was the only major port on the Pacific coast that had no Negro longshoremen. According to my informants, the opportunity to test Portland's anti-Negro position arose during World War II, after the shipping to American troops in the Pacific Theatre and to Russia brought the first shortage of longshoremen to the port since 1920. The left-wing radicals found one Negro who was willing to take the chance of infiltrating the exclusivist Portland Longshore Union. He began as a permit man with no real difficulty and was promoted to probationary membership. This form of probationary membership has long been abandoned, but it was a trial period and the candidate for full membership and registration as a regular longshoreman had to be brought before a membership meeting for approval after six months.

The man was apparently well accepted and enjoyed good personal relations with his fellow workers, and for this reason, the sponsoring left-wing faction felt no trepidation concerning his acceptance into full membership. They were in fact so confident that most of their leaders were not present at the meeting in which the Negro was to be accepted into Local 8.

Their confidence, however, was misplaced, for while they relaxed, certain that the first Negro candidate for membership in the Portland Local would not be seriously opposed, the numerically smaller right wing was bending every effort to block his entrance into the union. Both factions were depending strongly on the well-known attitude of the vast majority of Portland longshoremen: they simply did not care whether Negroes worked on the Portland waterfront or not. The question had never arisen before and overt opposition to the admission of Negroes had previously come only from the employers, which, after 1934, could have had no effect other than to dispose the longshoremen in favor of integration.

On the night that the first Negro candidate came before the membership for approval, the right wing had assembled every segregationist they could find and were well organized to dominate the meeting, which they did. My informants tell me that the right-wing tactic was to place speaker after speaker on the podium and to shout down everyone who attempted to defend the Negro. The outcome was inevitable: the Negro was rejected and the question of race, never previously of any importance, had been raised to the level of a real issue in Local 8.

The left wing was not disposed to accept this defeat, but the Negro candidate, undoubtedly frightened and humiliated, refused to return to the next membership meeting. The refusal of the Negro candidate to allow the left wing to force the issue of his admission into the union after they had organized their forces, a move which would probably have been successful, left them in a difficult position. They had assumed that they needed only one man to establish an integrationist policy in the local union, and had failed to insure against failure by recruiting more Negroes. As one of these men put it: "We put all of our eggs in one basket and then dropped it." Their original intention had been exactly reversed: instead of establishing a policy of integration, they had unintentionally helped to establish a policy of segregation, which could not be overcome until most of the older men had left the union (Record 1967).

Segregation, then, was the established policy of Local 8 in 1961, but as has been indicated, certain significant changes in the internal political structure of the union had taken place. The old factional lines had all but disappeared and a new factionalism based on age had emerged. Some predisposing events had taken place and the Local was at all times under pressure from the San Francisco headquarters of the International. In fact, the Local had already taken steps to integrate before

Harry Bridges first attempted to use the coercive power he had gained through the Mechanization and Modernization Contract. Negro members of other unions had been allowed to work on the Portland waterfront when their own unions were on strike and a few Negro visitors from other ports had been allowed to work in Portland. The major and decisive factor, however, was the shift in generations. It was the sons of the men who had turned down the first Negro candidate who admitted Negroes to the Portland waterfront in 1960, and it was these men who voted to place Negroes on the B list in 1963. This new factionalism almost dictated this policy simply as opposition to the policies of the older generation. One other serious obstacle remained: the tendency toward nepotism.

Nepotism Since the inception of the Portland Longshore Union in 1934, there had been two opposing internal tendencies. The left-wing ideology of the original organizers was firmly opposed to the natural tendency toward nepotism, but the main effect of their efforts was not to extinguish nepotism, but rather to limit it. Most of the left wing would have liked to have done away with any favoritism toward kin, and did manage to institute a lasting opposition to it. However, it was not until 1963, under the pressure of the International and civil rights groups that the Local finally adopted procedures and criteria for recruitment that completely precluded nepotism. Throughout the history of the Portland waterfront this had been the main factor in excluding Negroes from waterfront employment. Before 1941, there were not sufficient Negroes in the city to establish a tradition of black longshoremen, rather the original group had been white, and their desire to insure reasonable employment for their sons had automatically led to the exclusion of Negroes.

There was seldom a stated policy of nepotism, and in fact, the contrary was generally advocated, but when faced with the choice of giving work opportunity to a longshoreman's kinsman or to a nonkinsman, the preference had nearly always been given to the kinsman, and the final settlement of the problem of integration had bowed to this tradition.

OTHER PROBLEMS

Although at the time of this writing, there is no longer a race problem on the Portland waterfront, for a short period after the original decision to integrate, very serious problems arose and racial tension ran higher than it had since 1945. The nature of these problems and the way they were solved reveals much of how the longshoremen, both black and white, view the world. For in the final analysis, they are more alike than different. There are several reasons for these problems, and they do not fit well with many similar situations previously reported. Among the factors most prominent in segregation, economic competition has traditionally been the most important, but this is of little importance on the Portland waterfront, since the men who make the decisions as to whether or not to admit Negroes are in no way threatening their own economic positions by admitting them. Negroes do indeed compete with these men for economic goods (jobs) in the hiring hall, but this would be the case whether they were black or white, and the union has always carefully maintained its rolls at a level such that there has always been sufficient work for all regular longshoremen (A men).

Nonetheless, there was a rising resistance to admitting more Negroes and a growing feeling against Negroes. The factors contributing to this situation fall into two major categories, those resulting from the behavior of the new Negro longshoremen and those arising from the activities of others. In the former category there are the results of status rivalry among the black longshoremen and many unintentional violations of the symbolic behavior system of the other longshoremen by the Negroes. In the latter category there is one set of factors that has resulted in a direct challenge to the means by which legitimate status has traditionally been attained by new longshoremen: the procedures by which one becomes an A man or regular longshoreman and union member. These are highly interrelated and cannot be understood without reference to one another but they can be conceptually isolated for analysis. The first two factors, status rivalry among the black longshoremen and violations of the symbolic behavior system were by far the least important and only contribute to the grievances created by circumvention of the traditional means of acquiring legitimate status which was the central problem.

Status Rivalry   Status rivalry and differing sources of identification have caused a certain amount of anti-Negro feeling, primarily because the white longshoremen feel that there should be only one allegiance for all longshoremen, the Longshore Union and, thus, the longshore group. However, among the Negroes there was a tendency to label every man who had attained A status an "Uncle Tom," and for the men in the two categories (A and B) to differ more and more widely in their status orientations.

The ground on which this arose consists of the set of rules and criteria established by the union and the employers' association to avoid the possibility of racial discrimination among the B men. The recruitment system works in such a manner that a fairly large number of men receive B status at the same time (300 in 1964), and since men are placed on the A list as others retire from the industry, die, or leave for other occupations, not all of the B men are promoted to A status at the same time. For this reason, a point system was established based on such criteria as frequency of availability in the hiring hall to determine each man's place on the list. The man with the least number of points against him being first on the list and the man with the most points against him in the last position. If a man acquires enough points against himself, he is removed from the list by action of the Joint Labor Relations Committee.

Thus, each B man, through his own deportment and work performance, determines his own position on the B list relative to all other B men. The Negro B men separated eventually into two groups, one near the top of the list and the other near the bottom with some individuals ranged between. Those near the top became A men rather early and some at the bottom were discharged from the waterfront, and those who remained at the bottom of the list tended to believe that those who had become A men had in some way catered to the whites in order to attain that status. There was a difference between the two groups of Negroes, but it was a difference in status orientation. Those who were identified most strongly as members of the longshore group rather than as Negroes *per se* tended to be those who

A longshoreman at work covering up a hatch.

attained A status, while those who identified themselves most strongly with the black community had been those most frequently passed over for promotion. Those who were identified more as longshoremen tended to adopt the norms and attitudes of the white longshoremen including their work attitudes and thus presented better performance records, whereas those who rejected this identity with the whites may have injured their position by purposely refusing to comply with the work norms and thus acquired poor performance records.

Symbolic Behavior System   This is closely tied to violations of the symbolic behavior system. As I stated earlier (pages 26 and 27), the Portland longshoremen cherish their image as rough and tough individualists. Behavior that does damage to this image or appears to reject this identity on the part of another longshoreman is certain to be rejected by the overwhelming majority of longshoremen, which is one reason why they reject homosexuals. There are two forms of Negro behavior that constitute violations of this system. First and most obvious is what sounds very much like a southern accent to an Oregonian; and second is the manner in which some Negroes behave in the presence of whites.

The southern dialect of American English is a mark of low status in the Portland area, and is closely associated with the large numbers of southern workers imported during World War II to supply labor for the shipyards and other war industries. The southern migrants did not endear themselves to the citizens of Portland. The natives disliked their casual way of life and signified this by dubbing them "Okies" or more frequently "Hillbillies." These term carry connotations of laziness, lax morals, dirtiness, and a general lack of ambition. The dialect spoken by most Negroes closely approximates that of the southeastern portion of the United States to the undiscriminating ears of the Portlanders, and thus a certain amount of almost subconscious irritation is added to any interaction between the white and black longshoremen. I myself am irrationally affected by this dialect, even though I am conscious of the cause and make an effort to overcome it.

This linguistic difficulty in itself is, however, trivial except when combined with other forms of behavior that are objectionable to the longshoremen. Among them the most prominent are manner of dress and behavior that indicate a close identity with the black community. However, by far the most offensive behavior is a diffidence in dealing with whites that has been adopted by many Negroes as a defense against white prejudice. This diffidence often leads the other longshoremen to believe that the black longshoreman is lacking in the proper rough and tough attitude. Such an attitude, when combined with attire popular with Negroes, and the ghetto dialect, is enough to alienate the vast majority of white longshoremen. No one of these factors in itself is sufficient to lead to complete rejection as long as the man is a competent longshoreman or appears competent.

Some time before the Portland waterfront was officially integrated, a number of Negro pile bucks (a type of construction worker who works with pile drivers) were given special work cards and worked on the waterfront during a time when their own union was engaged in a strike. Few of the longshoremen objected to these tin-hatted, competent, and rather arrogant Negro workers. Although they spoke the ghetto dialect, in all other ways they fit well into the longshoremen's conception of how a longshoreman should look and act. They behaved in a cocky manner, were not at all slow to talk back, and performed the somewhat unfamiliar longshore work in a singularly competent fashion. Many of the new Negro long-shoremen conducted themselves in a like manner, but unfortunately there were a few who did not.

Legitimacy   The one most important factor that contributed to these racial tensions in the Portland Longshore Union was the question of legitimacy: the procedures by which a longshoreman gains A status. These procedures have been discussed at length under "Status Categories" in Chapter 5, but some reiteration will not be excessive. There are three status categories, A, B, and Y. A men are the fully registered union members with real job tenure; B men are somewhat in the position of apprentices, lacking full registration but bearing union permit cards and expecting to become A men in the course of time; the Y men have no official standing as longshoremen and have no expectations of becoming B or A men.

At one time the Y men were in the order of progression: one first became a Y man, then a B man, and eventually an A man. The terminology used to refer to these categories has changed from time to time, but the three categories and the concept of orderly progression from one to the other has been fairly stable since 1934. At no time since the formation of the union has any Portland long-shoreman become an A man without passing through the apprenticeship period or B status.

This progression was envisaged by the founders of the union, complete with the concept of membership approval of every new longshoreman, in order to guard against the corrupt hiring and recruitment procedures that had existed before the formation of the present union in 1934. The Portland longshoremen were and are aware of the problems of the New York waterfront and of the problems that had existed in Portland prior to 1934, and thus, any attempt to change or influence their recruiting and hiring procedures is viewed as thrusting the union toward the shape-up or the fink hall. Favoritism toward kinsmen has been a long standing tradition, but this operated primarily at the Y and B levels and was not important concerning promotion to the A list. At that point all candidates for A status and union membership must come before a stop-work (full) membership meeting and be either approved or rejected by the membership of the union.

In 1934, the union took upon itself the task of recruiting longshoremen and selecting among them in order to insure that the work force was composed of competent longshoremen, and it has done a fairly good job of fulfilling that respon-sibility over the years. Merely being a kinsman to some A man has never been sufficient grounds for admission to the A list. Kinsmen are as readily rejected as nonkinsmen, and sometimes, being kin to the wrong longshoreman is more of a liability than a credit to the candidate. The primary criterion for membership and A status has always been the individual's work record. Rarely has a man with a poor work record been admitted to A status.

It should be apparent that the sole means by which an individual can compile a work record is to work as a longshoreman, either as a Y or B man, before he is promoted to the A list, and the members of Local 8 are adamant on this point. They see this procedure as the only bulwark between themselves and their security and the conditions prevailing before 1934. In particular, there is a great fear of returning to a complete brother-in-law recruitment system.

When the Local commenced integration, pressure from the International Union and civil rights groups did not lessen but rather increased, and the pressure was always to place more Negroes on the A and B lists. This was the crux of the problem. The only way these demands could be met was to actively recruit Negroes for waterfront employment in preference to whites and members of other racial groups, and there was and is an ever-present fear that this would bring about the abandonment of their traditional promotion procedures and criteria.

Local 8 acquiesced to the original demand that they accept a quota of Negroes on the B list in 1964, and in fact they accepted every Negro who applied, on the grounds that it was necessary for them to do so in order to make up for past inequities and prove their good will. However, today, the vast majority of the Portland longshoremen feel that they have already atoned for the sins of the past and although genuinely willing to give all Negro applicants for B status fair treatment as individuals, they are not ready to accept another quota mandate.

There are, of course, other aspects to this problem. One of the most important is their fear of complete loss of their local autonomy and their democratic organization. This derives directly from the integration issue, since Harry Bridges and the International found a means to coerce the Portland Union through manipulation of the coast-wide registration procedures in a way that was by no means within the democratic tradition of the ILWU.

This has not been alleviated by the actions of some of the Negro B men, who have placed unfounded discrimination charges against the Local Union. These charges are based on the traditional dispatching procedures. Only A men have the contractual right to choose their jobs, but normally the B men are also allowed to pick the job they want from among those available. However, on peak days when there are a great many men to dispatch, and time is running short, the dispatchers may not allow the B men to pick their jobs so that they are on the job at starting time. The B men are dispatched after the A men. When there is a great deal of work and many men to dispatch, it may be uncomfortably close to starting time when the dispatchers finish hiring A men. Often under these circumstances, the dispatchers will "stack the pads" (place the hiring pads in a pile with the longest jobs on top and the shortest jobs on the bottom) so that the first man in the B board will receive the best job and the last man the worst. Unfortunately, this occurred on a morning when the first man in the B hiring board was a Negro, and a charge of discrimination resulted, because he was not allowed to choose his job.

This charge was not substantiated and was eventually dropped, and although most of the hard feelings generated by the incident have not quite been forgotten, they are fading fast. At this time all of the Negroes are members of the union and registered on the A list. Moreover, the current strike can have no effect other than to pull the black and white longshoremen more closely together.

7/The family

As I stated in the introduction, statistical data concerning the family life of the Portland longshoremen was not available to me. The longshoremen simply would not discuss their household affairs and many would not discuss their ancestry. This is a problem that is not familiar to many anthropologists, but it is a problem that will be faced by any researcher seeking family data among relatively affluent Americans. These Oregon longshoremen do not differ greatly from other well-to-do blue-collar workers, or, for that matter, from white-collar workers or professionals in their attitudes toward their families and households. Indeed, the most striking thing about their attitudes toward their families and about the families themselves is their unremarkable nature.

In this area of my research I was forced to fall back on my many years of association with longshoremen and their families, and the generalizations and examples set down here are for the most part drawn from my own long experience within the Portland longshore group. Again, the families do not differ greatly from those of many other Americans, but there are certain accents on behavior and somewhat distinctive attitudes that I have noted.

The whole family structure and the associated attitudes are old-fashioned and would seem most in place in a small midwestern farm town. There is a great deal of informal interaction between kinsmen even though they do not tend to live in close proximity to one another, which is quite apparent from the residence pattern (see Figure 1). Association is not biased toward either the husband's or the wife's family, but the wife's family is probably the focus of more interaction than the husband's primarily because the women are less likely to be immigrants to the area than are the men. Visiting is extremely informal. Family members tend to call on one another without advance notice whenever the urge strikes them. No special occasion is necessary to precipitate a visit, but more formalities are likely to be observed on occasions such as birthdays, anniversaries, and important holidays. Christmas and crises such as a death in the family often are the occasions for extremely large family gatherings. At one funeral I attended there were over sixty kinsmen present, several of whom had come from distant locations, and a large number of longshoremen who were not relatives were also present.

Informal visits normally take place in the kitchen, which is the place where friends and family are usually entertained. Although there is an increasing move toward the living room and the television set, the kitchen is still the prime gathering place for the family, and thus the longshoremen are inclined to prefer big old houses with large kitchens. Close friends and family members ordinarily enter the house through the back door which is, in most cases, also the kitchen door, but others are required to use the front door and are entertained in the living room. It is not unusual for close family members and friends to enter the house with no more than perfunctory notice: they may knock or otherwise announce their presence but often do not wait for the door to be opened or an invitation to enter. Interaction on these occasions often seems superficial. Conversation tends to center around the job or union affairs, the family car, proposed home construction, and sports among the men, and around family affairs and children among the women. The purpose of a visit is seldom to exchange or impart information, but rather to be in the presence of family members: the visit is an end in itself and not a means to an end.

SEX AND MARRIAGE

From the longshoreman's viewpoint, one is not fully a man until he is married and has taken on the responsibility of a family. Men who do not marry or who fail to accept the obligations of the marital estate are universally regarded as immature. Unmarried longshoremen are rare in the extreme, partially because of the unwillingness of the group to take a single man seriously, that is, they regard him as a "kid"; and very importantly because of the heavy value placed on rearing children. Consensual unions, although rare, are not unknown, and most of the cases that I observed ended in formal marriage. The children enter into this also. I know of one case where a man maintained such a union for many years, as he stated, because his common-law wife was very good for the children that he was left to raise from a previous marriage. The only other permanent consensual union of which I am aware involved a longshoreman whose legal wife had mistreated the man's children so badly that he not only left her but gained legal custody of the children, not an easy task under Oregon law; and he seemed fearful of entering formally into marriage again.

I lack a proper sample to indicate the frequency of divorce within the group, but it would seem to be nearly the same as the national average. This information would not indicate anything of very great importance even if I did have such a sample, for it is not whether or not one is ever divorced that indicates attitudes toward marriage, or the strength of a value on stable marriage. To the contrary, many young people, inside and outside the longshore group, divorce one spouse after only a short period and then engage in a more permanent union. The information that indicates the presence of a strong value on stable marriage is the great number of couples who have been married for several decades, and the expressed attitudes of group members toward particular cases of marriage breakdown. Indeed, all of the older men whom I interviewed had been married to the same woman for many years, with the exception of a few widowers. One man had been married three times simply because his two previous wives had died. This does not tell us much about the younger generation, but in my own long experience within the group, I detected little change in this basic old-fashioned attitude.

The group is very old-fashioned in nearly all of their attitudes toward marriage and sex. I do not mean to imply that their attitude toward sex is a puritanical one, for I can only recall a very few people in my whole experience who did not have a very realistic attitude toward the subject. In many ways, this configuration is very rural. It is difficult indeed to conceal the mechanical aspects of sex from a rural child who from an early age has seen animals breeding. Moreover, ancient folk truisms are rife within the group. I cannot, of course, say what was passed on from mother to daughter, since I was systematically excluded from this realm of knowledge; but the older men, kinsmen and nonkinsmen, pass on the group attitudes toward sex and marriage through the use of folk saws and explicit instruction. I do not remember how old I was when I first heard the saying, "A hard dick has no conscience," but I was very young. Perhaps the implications of this piece of crude folk wisdom are not clear, without explanation. It indicates that a man is usually thoughtless when sexually aroused; however, it carries the implication that he should not be at other times. Illicit sex is itself not considered inherently evil, unless it leads to evil consequences, such as a man's disregarding his family responsibilities in favor of his sexual proclivities. Moreover, I was explicitly instructed by my father and admonished by many others to care for my family, regardless of the circumstances. I was also clearly told that a pregnancy produced by my sex drive was my responsibility and that my family would not support me in any attempt to deny the consequences of my actions.

Nor is a man encouraged to discuss his wife or her faults publicly. Although the longshoremen frequently praise the homely virtues of their wives, such as their thrift or industry, I have never heard a longshoreman, except in a few cases where the marriage was already dissolved, criticize his wife or discuss their deeper personal relationship. It is noteworthy that I have never heard one of these men claim that he loved his wife, nor express personal affection toward any member of his family, except occasionally to boast at intolerable lengths of their accomplishments, especially those of their sons. The fact, however, that most of these men remain with the same woman for many years and appear content indicates clearly that there are deep affective ties between themselves and their wives, and that these ties are significant in their lives. Although I have never heard one of them claim virtue for it, they appear to be amazingly faithful to their wives, in light of their public image.

This reticence concerning emotions on the part of a group of very outspoken males derives from a deeply seated belief that verbally expressed emotions lack depth and sincerity. In other words, they regard protestations of undying love as cheap and insincere, especially if publicly voiced. Such things are private matters between two people in the case of a man and his wife, and it is taken as a matter of course that does not need verbal expression that one cares deeply for one's children.

The devil-may-care roughneck image maintained by the longshoremen requires that they flatter and flirt with almost every reasonably attractive woman that they encounter other than kinswomen or other men's wives. This flirtation is, however, not meant to be taken seriously. When it is taken seriously and has been favorably received, the longshoreman's usual reaction is to flee to his home. There are, however, a few well-known "chippies" (men that take any sexual opportunities that they encounter) in the group, but although the other longshoremen view their activities with a kind of amused tolerance, they are neither encouraged nor admired. I have heard more than one of these men whose sexual exploits led to a divorce refer to himself as a "damn fool" and to his sexual activities as "damn foolishness." The other longshoremen heartily concur with these opinions, and there is little doubt that even the "chippies" subscribe to the group norms that condemn their activities.

The female members of a longshoreman's family are treated with almost exaggerated respect by the other longshoremen. At one time, I left a young woman outside the longshore hall while I went in to conduct a few minutes' business. The young woman was familiar with the colorful reputation of the longshoremen and had hoped to observe some of their behavior. However, she was sitting on my motorcycle, and was, therefore, considered possibly a member of my family. She reported to me later that, although some fifty of the longshoremen walked past her, the only ones who so much as looked at her were two men in their early sixties who inquired as to her comfort.

CAUSES FOR DIVORCE

Among the causes for divorce, interference with the domestic household by the wife's family, infidelity on the part of the husband, excessive drinking, financial irresponsibility, and sexual incompatibility were among the reasons for marital breakdown that I have heard mentioned. I believe that if infidelity on the wife's part had been a cause, it would not have been mentioned and, undoubtedly, other less straightforward reasons were often simply not voiced. Laziness or lack of economy on the wife's part was the complaint voiced most often when a marriage was in the process of dissolution, but this was probably very often a simple cover for other complaints.

It is notable that strife over finances was seldom mentioned, since this is usually reported as the major focus of strain in blue-collar families (Hurvitz 1964). There are, however, several cogent reasons for the lack of this problem in longshore families. Chief among these is the security of waterfront employment and the affluence of the longshore group which derive from the nature and activities of the union. Waterfront employment is irregular, but there are no periodic lay-offs of the work force, and, thus, savings are not periodically depleted nor is there ever a need to leave the city or state to seek employment as is often the case with factory and other blue-collar workers. A West Coast longshoreman is assured of job tenure for as long as he may wish to continue working on the waterfront, and, with rare exceptions, these longshoremen stay in the industry until retired.

This makes for the establishment of deep local roots and the construction of widely ramified family networks, which again contribute to the financial and marital stability of the longshoremen. These ramified family networks (see Figure 6) offer not only the satisfactions normally derived from association with kinsmen but also the very real possibility of financial or other assistance when it is needed. The relatively homogeneous nature of the city of Portland and the state of Oregon contributes to marital and family stability. In such a homogeneous context, it is very unlikely that the longshoreman and his wife will have dissimilar family backgrounds, and the probability that their expectations of one another's role performances will agree is very much augmented. This probability is furthered by the high degree of *de facto* endogamy.

THE CONJUGAL FAMILY

The conjugal unit is not unusual for an American family, and nearly always consists of only the married couple and their children. I know of no case where grandparents are resident in the home, although there may be a few such household units. The conjugal family and indeed the entire family structure is reminiscent of a Midwestern farm family, which is not surprising in the light of the recent Midwestern rural derivation of most of the citizens of Portland.

As in most American families, the role of the longshoreman husband is that of the family provider, and his home and much of the family activity are oriented around his needs as the primary economic producer. My impression is that, although the pattern is very much like that of other American families, there is a somewhat greater emphasis placed on the central role of the longshoreman husband and father than there is in other families. Perhaps it is best defined in contrast to that of his wife than it is in many family structures, and his role in respect to his contribution to the family welfare is very clearly defined: he is expected to provide a fair level of economic support for his family, to attend to the physical discipline of the children, and to maintain the house and yard.

The longshoreman's family is very aware of the arduous and hazardous nature of his work and believe that he needs special care and consideration in order to meet the difficult demands of his job. It is of course not true that all longshoremen engage in arduous labor or work on dangerous jobs at all times, but they do not seem to feel that it is necessary to bring this to the attention of their wives, nor do they feel obliged to mention the many satisfactions, social and other, that they derive from their work. Rather, they prefer to reap the benefits of their image. Few longshoremen would consider preparing their own breakfast or engaging in other household work so long as their wives were able to do so or they had daughters capable of performing these tasks.

On the other hand, I am familiar with two cases where longshoremen performed all the household work as well as working full time on the waterfront. In one case, the man's wife had died and left him with two small children to raise. This man had no relatives within the longshore group or the city upon whom he could call for assistance. Consequently, although he had a problem with drinking, he raised his family without assistance. He did not, however, provide for them as well as most longshoremen like to provide for their families. Normally, men who do not provide more than a minimal living for their dependents, and they are rare, are frequently and openly criticized by the other longshoremen. This custom brings a great deal of social pressure to bear on those men who are negligent of their families. In the light of his special difficulties, however, this widower was not criticized but, rather, praised for continuing his efforts.

The vast majority of the longshoremen and their families believe that some forms of otherwise disvalued behavior, such as occasionally getting drunk, are excusable on the grounds that the longshoremen work hard and need to "let go" once in a while, but steady drinking and the failure to provide for one's family is not so readily forgiven. On the other hand, the statement that a man has always taken good care of his family or that his wife has never had to work to help support the family will excuse many types of untoward behavior within the longshore group. Even "chippy-chasing" (illicit sexual behavior) is often excused on these grounds.

Another man who has managed to hold together and care for his family in the face of great difficulties is the subject of somewhat greater admiration from the other longshoremen because he has never succumbed to the temptation to lighten his problems with alcohol. This man's wife was stricken with a disease akin to muscular dystrophy when he was twenty-six years of age. At that time he had four small children ranging from one to six years of age. His wife's condition rendered her unable to care for the children or to do even light housework. In addition to this, she needed special care for which he could not afford to pay. Thus, for the last ten years, he has done most of the housework, cared for his children, cooked the family meals, and acted as part-time nurse for his wife as well as working full-time on the waterfront. In fact, this man's earnings have normally been among the top ten in the port for the entire period.

It is, however, quite clear that he could not maintain his house or his children in more than a minimal fashion. He has always provided more than sufficient funds, but in order to do this he has had to work six days per week and has not had the time or energy to keep his house in proper condition or to tend to his children properly. Thus, the house is generally not very clean or well kept and his children are anything but well groomed, although they have never wanted for sufficient food or clothing, or adequate shelter, nor have they been neglected by their father, since he spends what little spare time he has with his children.

He has been urged by public agencies to give up his family for the welfare of all involved, but such suggestions have only served to drive him to greater efforts and to acquire several rather vicious dogs to keep outsiders away from his home. His efforts have not gone unnoticed on the waterfront, since his situation is well-known among the other men. Although the other longshoremen are appalled by the magnitude of his difficulties they stand somewhat in awe of his energy and stamina, and he is admired for clinging so tenaciously to his family under circumstances where he might understandably have given it up. However, although this man's stamina is outstanding, his devotion to his family is not; it is merely a fair example of the regard in which most longshoremen hold their families.

The impression must not be given that there are no longshoremen who do not adequately provide for their families. There are about twenty-eight such men known to me in the Portland longshore group, and all but one of these men are notorious drunks. In fact, this number will include all of the drunks on the Portland waterfront. It is not, however, true that the families of all these men suffer from insufficient funds for some of them have a certain amount of inherited money, in some cases their wives have an outside income, and in others the wives work to support the family and their husband's thirsts. Some of these men have been divorced because of their drinking habits (five to my knowledge), but for the most part their wives have remained with them. The behavior of these men is not supported by the other longshoremen, but they are usually so far gone that they are "rummies" and not really aware of the disapproval of the other men.

The conjugal family unit is very much an economic unit and the chief role of the wife is to assist her husband in maintaining the economic welfare of the family. Her economic role is recognized by the men, and it is often commented that "a woman will make you or break you." She must help balance the uneven weekly funds brought in by her husband and economize on household expenditures when the financial situation is tight because the possibility that it will remain tight for a time is always present. Many longshoremen retain only necessary expense money from their weekly checks and give the rest to their wives whose responsibility it is to pay the bills and set some of the money aside for periods when it is less plentiful. Others may deposit a set amount in the credit union before dividing the remaining money with their wives, and there are of course other variations on this pattern. Many of the men will claim that they handle all the finances of the family, but it is well known that this is more bravado than fact; and such a claim is often met with derision.

The planning of large, long-term investments is usually undertaken by both husband and wife, although a man may sometimes put forth the claim that he should make the final decision because he has earned or will earn the money to pay for the item. On the other hand, the great majority of longshoremen take a deep interest in the condition of their homes and will generally concur in the opinion of their wives as to what may be needed in the way of large appliances such as built-in ovens, dishwashers, refrigerators and the like. In the selection of which particular brand of appliance to purchase among the many varieties, the husband usually makes the decision on the basis of his superior knowledge of and experience with mechanical contrivances.

CHILDREN

The conjugal family is unusually parent controlled and dominated in contrast to the child centered middle-class family. Children are not allowed to interfere in adult activities, must always submit to parental decisions, and may not contradict or defy their parents or other adults. However, in another sense, the children are very much the center of the family in that their interests are always considered by their parents before any action that will affect them or their welfare is initiated. The major difference between this family and the typical middle-class "child-centered" family lies in the theory of child training. The longshoremen and their wives have seldom come in contact with modern theories of child training, and most of those who have express a low opinion of their efficacy and disagree with their basic premises.

The use of physical punishment is part of this complex and is based on the theory that physical punishment is not revenge or an occasion for venting parental emotions but a lesson for life, because the larger society, like the family, has laws and rules any infringement of which is certain to bring punishment that may not only be physical, but that is in many ways more painful than that administered by the child's parents. Thus, it is the parents' duty to punish the child in a manner sufficiently stern that the child will be permanently impressed with the necessity and desirability of avoiding the commission of violations of family or societal laws. Children below the ages of four to six years are ordinarily not spanked because it is believed that they will not understand the reasons for the punishment.

Affection toward their children, like punishment, is physically but seldom verbally displayed. Children are often brought into the hiring hall on payday and shown the intricacies of the hiring process by their fathers at an early age. Small children are so frequently in the hiring hall that one earnings clerk kept a sack of candy in his office which he distributed to visiting children. Affection toward young children is displayed physically by holding them or, in the case of older boys, by roughhousing. The longshoreman's irregular work regime allows him to spend more time with his children than most workers, and the longshoremen tend to take maximum advantage of this circumstance. Moreover, children, especially the boys, are often taken aboard the ships and onto the docks by their fathers. It is not unusual to see a crane or winch operator accompanied by his son while working, and nearly all of the longshoremen take their families on occasional tours of the ships and docks.

Responsibility for a child's welfare does not totally end when the child becomes an adult, and a considerable amount of planning for the child's career is normal. There is an increasing awareness that there will not be sufficient employment opportunity on the waterfront for their sons and that many similar occupations are not likely to be available in the near future. Many now recognize that other preparations must be made if their children are to prosper. Their daughters are expected to marry, but increasingly they are sent to college and business school so that they need not depend on marriage or their husband's longevity. The boys are urged to obtain some variety of practical training that will fit them to earn an adequate livelihood and are often subsidized while attending school or working their way into a good job. There is very little concern here with social standing but a great concern with the earnings potential and security of a chosen trade. Many of the younger longshoremen have some college training and quite a few have degrees in elementary or secondary education, because it is felt that there will always be a need for school teachers. But because of the low income associated with teaching, these degrees serve only as insurance against hard times or disability.

INTERRELATIONSHIP IN THE LONGSHORE GROUP

The degree of relationship among members of the longshore group is very high. On a count of the 1964 B list more than half of the B men were consanguines of other men on the A or B lists, and the same proportion appeared on a count of a sample of the A list. Consanguineal kinsmen are not difficult to identify, but the intricacies of affinal ties are not only more difficult but appear to be extensive and could not be fully explored with the resources at my disposal. Just how exten-sive these ties are would be difficult to even estimate, but that they are very exten-sive is revealed by some of the genealogies collected. Moreover, almost every light conversation with a longshoreman tended to reveal yet another affinal set. Con-sanguineal and affinal kinsmen then probably account for something like seventy percent or more of the longshore group.

There are several reasons for this high degree of interrelationship. Nepotism within the union and the longshore industry is certainly an important factor, but will not alone account for the large number of longshoremen's sons on the 1964 B list. By 1964, new recruitment procedures resulting from the Taft–Hartley Act and the integration crisis had made nepotism all but impossible. Indeed, it is doubtful in the extreme that nepotism played any part. A high rate of recruitment among longshoremen's kinsmen has, in part, always been due to well maintained lines of communications among the tight-knit longshore families. Any decision to recruit new B men must be discussed and voted on in a meeting of the union before it can be put into action. This precedes the actual advertisement for new men by some time, and during this period the union members inform those of their relatives who are interested in waterfront employment. Other persons can only discover that applications for B men are being taken by reading the legally required newspaper advertisements. Many other persons may be interested in waterfront employment, but if they are not consistent readers of the local news-papers, they will probably not see the advertisements. The net result is that the majority of applicants are related to longshoremen, and almost any method of selecting among the applicants is certain to produce a preponderance of men related to longshoremen.

The high degree of association with longshoremen who are not kinsmen also fosters the high frequency of kin ties within the group. Informal visiting brings the longshoremen into contact with the sisters and daughters of other longshore-men and many marriages result from these contacts. Another factor that contri-butes to the ramification of kinship ties is the tendency of migrants and other newcomers to the group to bring their relatives and friends to the waterfront. Among the Negroes admitted to B status in 1964, several are related to one an-other, and this, of course, is the beginning of the sort of kinship network that characterizes the entire group as illustrated in Figures 2 and 3.

8 / Extra-work activities: adaptations to an irregular work regime

In response to the erratic nature of waterfront employment and the consequent irregular income and relatively unpredictable pattern of leisure time, the longshoremen have developed a number of adaptations, both in terms of the development of secondary sources of income and leisure activities. The union and hiring system, as stated earlier, are also very much a part of this set of adaptations as is the devil-may-care roughneck image projected by the longshoremen. There are both advantages and disadvantages to the irregular nature of waterfront employment, and the longshoreman's attitudes and behavior are tailored to take maximum advantage of the first and greatly minimize the second. The central aspect of their adaptation is characterized by the feast-or-famine philosophy.

THE FEAST-OR-FAMINE PHILOSOPHY

The core of the feast-or-famine philosophy is that it is best to work when employment is plentiful and take one's leisure when it is not. In order to do this the longshoreman must show up in the hiring hall whenever there is any chance of obtaining employment, which means almost every day. If he doesn't get a job he can then engage in other activities. He may, of course choose not to show up when there is plentiful employment but this is a matter of balancing economic necessity against the desire to engage in other activities. Due to the nature of the union and the hiring system, there is no penalty for not working other than the loss of pay, and thus there is no goad to make him go to the hiring hall other than economic necessity. This calls for a kind of extreme self discipline; he cannot slip into the established regime of a five day work week. He must decide for himself how often he needs work if he is to earn an appropriate living for himself and his family. Although they are fond of their "I don't give a damn" image, their yearly earnings, real estate holdings, and the healthy state of their credit union indicate that the Portland longshoremen do indeed calculate these matters very carefully. There is a certain deep appeal in being in control of one's own work regime and financial affairs, but its price is iron self-discipline and the willingness to face the possibility of economic disaster. The devil-may-care image of self discussed on page 21 is also very much a part of this philosophy, for it is by means of this presentation of self that the longshoreman communicates his ability to handle whatever problems, physical or financial, that may arise. The maintenance of this image entails rigid self-discipline, for if an individual were not able to control his actions in a way that allowed him to balance desire against economic necessity, it would soon be obvious to all, and the spurious nature of his claim to the rough-neck identity could not be maintained.

Obviously, the actual leisure time derived from the irregularity of the work regime is put to some use. A good deal of it is used for family recreation which contributes to well integrated domestic units, but it is also utilized for economic gain.

SECONDARY SOURCES OF INCOME

The Portland longshoremen have developed several secondary sources of income that can be activated during low periods on the waterfront. Foremost among these are stump ranching, real estate rentals and investments, the operation of small businesses and the economic utilization of personal skills. Moonlighting, working at another job, is scarcely tenable in light of the unpredictable nature of the long-shoreman's work day and the unsympathetic stance of the local union toward it. These activities are many and varied and do not follow the usual pattern of the blue-collar business man in terms of behavior or motivation. Longshoremen do not usually wish to leave the waterfront, but rather wish to bolster their incomes and contribute further to the economic welfare of their families.

The Stump Ranch   The prime example of this sort of activity is "stump ranching." This form of subsistence farming was originally practiced by persons who bought up logged off land at very low prices and cleared the stumps of the big trees in their spare time while working at some job from which they made their livelihood. The term "stump rancher" has been extended to include anyone who is working full time at some occupation other than farming and uses his free time to improve his marginal land. This form of farming has been much criticized as uneconomical, but the criticism has generally been from a profit-oriented viewpoint (Anastasio 1960). The stump ranch does contribute economi-cally to the owner, but the gain is, for the most part, long term and, at least ini-tially, not a cash profit.

The stump rancher usually builds a house on his property and from this he realizes his first gain: rent-free housing. In the case of the longshoreman, the house is usually built in quite an economical manner, since many, and often all, of the building materials, are legitimately or otherwise obtained from the water-front. Furthermore, the stump rancher invariably builds the house himself. Some of these houses are surprisingly well built and modern, and one of the best was built almost entirely from materials derived from the docks, including the marble facing for a huge fireplace. Less often now but frequently in the recent past, after enough of the house was completed so that the longshoreman and his family could move into it, a chicken house was constructed and stocked and a large garden was planted, fertilized by manure from the chicken house. As soon as possible enough additional livestock was purchased to make the stump ranch self-supporting, and the longshoreman and his family would raise nearly all of the food they consumed. This form of subsistence farming is a thing of the past in most parts of the country, but is still very much a Northwestern institution (Anastasio 1960).

Often the one-time stump ranch is completely cleared and the owner has a productive truck farm in addition to his subsistence farm. Unexpected financial success has come to some of the local stump ranchers because of the growth of the city. Land that was purchased twenty years ago for a few dollars an acre is now being subdivided and sold at prices in excess of one thousand dollars per building lot. A profit of about fifty thousand dollars was realized from one such investment.

Real Estate   The investment in real estate is thought to be the best possible investment and many longshoremen have invested in real estate within the city. Short term profit is not usually the incentive for investing in real estate, and many longshoremen have bought houses within the city on a small down payment and paid for them with the incoming rents. Many of these men have become landlords on a scale that almost matches that of some of the local Italian garbagemen who have become some of the largest landowners in the city. Older houses that may be purchased cheaply are bought up (and rented out at rents barely sufficient to pay the taxes and maintenance) near the growing industrial areas of the city, with the almost certain expectation that the value of the property will greatly increase as it becomes industrial rather than residential. There are a few cases of men who own business property such as store buildings and a small but significant number of men who own small apartment buildings and motels.

Crafts   Another form of economic activity that is not concerned with real estate is the part-time business carried on by some of the men who are skilled workers and craftsmen. One of the Portland longshoremen was a skilled gunsmith. His shop was located in the basement of his home and he drew most of his business from among the longshoremen, not because his rates were lower than those of other local gunsmiths, but because they felt he could be trusted not to cheat them and to do a good job. The same proposition holds for several other skilled men such as auto mechanics and television and radio repairmen. These part-time businesses require almost no capital investment other than the hand tools and equipment that the business requires. The business is usually conducted in the home or garage and no hired personnel are necessary.

A few men work part-time at other jobs, but the union's strong negative position concerning "moonlighting" keeps them to a minimum. There are a few men who race motorcycles, and perhaps two wrestlers in the longshore group. These activities are so irregular that they do not come under the union's ban, and can be carried on as long as the individual is capable of performing. One of these men stated that he earned his living on the waterfront and "paid for his Cadillac wrestling."

Entrepreneurship   Another set of activities engaged in by a fairly large number of longshoremen are akin to the activities of the Yankee trader: the buying and selling of almost anything that will turn a profit. Usually this involves only small merchandise and used automobiles, but it sometimes develops into a large scale business enterprise. One of these men started his business career with a fruit stand during World War II. He made a success of the fruit stand which was operated mostly by his family and then sold it when the competition tightened at the end of the war. His next venture was in the used truck business. He purchased a number of surplus army trucks and converted them into logging trucks. The automotive industry was still not meeting the demand for automobiles and trucks, and again this individual made a considerable profit and quit the business when new equipment became readily available. At the same time, he had several other enterprises underway, and had accumulated an estimated $200,000 in cash and property. He then became entangled in legal difficulties and supposedly lost everything and was left with a judgment of about $70,000 against his future earnings. Through various subterfuges he overcame these problems and continued dealing in sundry small merchandise and then began to build houses to sell. He is still building homes and engaging in other mercantile activities while working full-time on the waterfront. Few men have been as successful as this longshoreman, but his pattern of behavior is not extraordinary.

Operating Businesses   Going into a business, such as a store, restaurant, or garage is not typical of the Portland longshoremen, although there are several men who own bars and restaurants. These men, however, do not leave the waterfront to go into business. These businesses are usually operated by the longshoreman's wife or some other family member, although there are men who have hired managers to run their bars. The normal pattern here is not to attempt to establish a new enterprise, but to purchase a business that is in operation and is doing well. The fact that these men continue to work on the waterfront contributes to the success of their businesses: additional capital is obtained by working more than usual when it is required, and since they do not depend on the business for a livelihood, it can be operated on a very slim profit margin for a considerable period of time. There are a few men who fish commercially during the season, but their numbers have declined rapidly in the last two decades.

MOTIVATIONS

The pattern of longshore economic enterprise carried on outside of the context of their occupation is quite different from that usually described for blue-collar workers who attempt to go into business for themselves in order to escape the drudgery of their jobs, to gain security from the ever-present threat of the lay-off, and to advance themselves socially (Mayer and Goldstein 1964). The longshoremen's motives are almost entirely confined to contributing to the economic welfare of the family. The drive for security plays its part and is very much interwoven with the powerful value placed on the ownership of land. Partially, these activities are remnants of the frontier practice of engaging in "multiple alternative and part-time occupations" (Anastasio 1960:23), a pattern that was an absolute necessity on the frontier. Although the frontier is gone, some of its conditions such as the lack of manufacturing industries and many of the attitudes and values it engendered remain.

Unlike the blue-collar worker described by Mayer and Goldstein, the Portland longshoreman seldom "goes into business." He usually operates a part-time enterprise that requires very little in the way of investment in equipment or inventory. In the one case cited above where the man actually went into business several times, he had no intention of staying in the business, until his last venture. The other businesses were meant to be short term affairs. He entered into a business when demand was extremely high and supply equally short and left the business as soon as competition developed.

SOCIAL MOBILITY

The Portland longshoremen do not engage in business for the purpose of social advancement: they do not aspire to social position. Social position and the prestige derived from it are meaningless to them; however, personal accomplishments as reflected in the accrual of material wealth have deep meaning. To the longshoremen, advancement means economic advancement, and this is the goal toward which they strive. Investing in real estate, building a business, or acquiring an education that can lead to economic advancement are seen as real equivalents. Striving toward other goals (i.e., seeking prestige in the eyes of the wider community) is viewed as wasted effort and therefore disvalued (Miller and Riessman, 1964).

EDUCATION

The typical longshore attitude toward education beyond the high school level is negative, unless it contributes in some way to the material welfare of the individual and his family. Visible occupations such as those of lawyers, medical doctors, engineers, and the like, that are believed to be more remunerative than longshoring are considered worthwhile goals and men who acquire the necessary education to attain such positions are admired for their drive and ambition. Indeed, the longshore union encourages men who are seeking higher education by allowing them great leeway in their roles as longshoremen. Longshoremen who are attending medical school, dental school, law school, or otherwise seeking an education to fit them for another occupation are allowed to work when they wish, and the restriction that a longshoreman must work once every thirty days in order to remain on the registration list is circumvented through established formal procedures. This privilege was extended to me when I was attending Portland State College and the University of Illinois, and without this advantage I could not have acquired an advanced education.

There are a number of institutions of higher education in the Portland area including Reed College, the University of Portland, Portland State College, the University of Oregon Medical and Dental Schools, a number of smaller colleges and several law schools. The facilities for obtaining a higher education are in other words plentifully available in the Portland area; however, many of these institutions are felt to be prohibitively expensive and would not allow the very loose scheduling necessary for a longshoreman to attend them. The children of a number of longshoremen have been educated in these schools, but many families simply cannot afford them. The other alternative was the extension center of the University of Oregon, which became Portland State College in the 1950s and a degree granting institution in 1955. This presented an economically feasible opportunity for many longshore families, and many of their children have attended Portland State since that time. It also presented an opportunity for many of the younger longshoremen who had wished to acquire an education. For some of them it also presented an economic opportunity: some men holding B status found they could attend the college as full-time students and collect veterans' benefits while working as longshoremen and thus supplement their earnings.

Statistical data on the educational level of the Portland longshoremen is not available, but it apparently has risen considerably over the years. Many of the old time longshoremen were illiterate and I do not believe that any of the present day longshoremen have not had at least an elementary education. Moreover, men applying for B status are now required to have a high school education, and a considerable number of the younger men have college degrees or have attended college. An estimate of at least 10% would not seem excessive, but the significance of this relatively high proportion of educated longshoremen is much diminished when compared with the level of education of the state and the city in general: Oregon has one of the highest levels of educational attainment in the country. In other words, the longshoremen, in terms of education, would seem to present only a cross section of the state as they do in terms of ethnic composition.

The most noteworthy aspect of the level of education within the group is that so many of the educated men remain on the waterfront. The reason for this is not complex: a BA or BS degree will not usually allow an individual to obtain a position that will yield a better income than he would derive from longshoring, and it cannot be overemphasized that these men are not greatly interested in the attainment of prestige or social advancement at the cost of economic loss. The majority of positions that are open to individuals with only four years of college often pay considerably less than longshoring and will not allow the same manipulation of working and leisure time. However, acquiring a degree in a field such as education where it is felt that there will always be an opportunity for employment is regarded as a sort of insurance against hard times on the waterfront such as might be brought on by another depression, or the loss of union power and the imposition of some control which would render waterfront employment undesirable to many of these men.

Thus, the Portland longshoremen take full advantage of the educational resources of the area in a manner determined by their attitudes, values, and personal abilities and interests. This is advantageous not only to individuals but to the group and especially to the union because of the growing complexity of labor relations and collective bargaining contracts. More and more frequently men are elected to office in the union who have college educations, which may enhance the position of the union in collective bargaining with college-trained employer representatives. At this time most of the salaried officials have at least some college education and several have degrees.

LEISURE ACTIVITIES

The longshoremen's extra-work economic activities differ from those of other blue-collar workers both in the nature of the enterprises which they undertake and in the motivation behind these activities. However, most of their leisure time is spent in much the same way as that of other blue-collar workers and their motivations do not seem to differ widely.

Few of the Portland longshoremen belong to any organization other than the ILWU, and nearly all of their past organizational affiliations have been with the armed forces. Lodge membership was at one time more extensive than it is today because of the insurance features of many lodges. The growth of insurance benefits within the union and collective bargaining contexts has, however, greatly reduced lodge membership. Few of the longshoremen belong to voluntary associations, and those who do are for the most part members of various kinds of sports clubs and other organizations concerned with outdoor activities, such as the Sidewinder Motorcycle Club (American Motorcycle Association).

The Portland longshoremen spend the greatest amount of their leisure time, when they are not engaged in economic activities, in or near their homes, puttering in the garden, improving the lawn and landscaping, and painting or otherwise improving their homes. Driving around the city or the surrounding countryside with the family and enjoying the abundant Oregon scenery is another favorite pastime for the longshoremen.

During the hunting season, there is invariably a shortage of longshoremen in the port. A number of men take their vacations at that time, in order to go hunting. These hunting trips are usually family affairs: many of the men take their wives and older children with them. The trout fishing season does not deplete the work force as drastically as the deer and elk seasons because good trout fishing is available closer to Portland and many of the fishermen do not take the whole family along on every fishing trip. However, when Portland gangs are ordered to coastal ports, such as Newport, many of the longshoremen gather up their families and take advantage of the opportunity to indulge in ocean fishing.

Actually, most of the hunting, fishing trips, or camping trips are family outings for which the sport is a rationalization. They are activities which allow the father to indulge in his favorite sport while permitting the whole family to get out together in the open and away from the city. Obviously, young women with very small children cannot accompany their husbands so freely, but many leave the children with grandparents on these occasions. As the longshoreman becomes more affluent with advancing age, he commonly owns two vehicles: a truck or station wagon that is used for work and camping and an automobile, often a large and expensive vehicle such as a Thunderbird. The car is normally used by his wife or when the family takes long trips.

The rockhound is a transform of the hunter. His hobby carries him even further afield than does that of the hunter, and it requires an even greater outlay in terms of machinery. Aside from the lapidary equipment necessary to his avocation, he often owns a Jeep and some sort of small, powerful motorcycle to take him into places where the Jeep cannot go. Again, his expeditions are often family affairs and differ little from those of the hunter.

There are many other forms of outdoor sports in which Portland longshoremen engage, such as motorcycle racing, horseback riding, skiing, waterskiing, boating, swimming, hiking, golfing, and even birdwatching. But none of them are quite the family affairs or are as widespread as are fishing and hunting. The one generalization that can be made about the leisure activities of the Portland longshoremen is that they are predominantly outdoor activities. However, outdoor activities are not always feasible. Oregon winters are not very cold, but they are featured by a great deal of rather steady precipitation which can make outdoor activities less than enjoyable.

Indoor leisure activities are less strenuous than outside activities, and much time is spent watching others engage in sports when inclement weather prohibits such activities for sportsminded longshoremen. Visiting relatives and other longshoremen takes up a considerable amount of time, and a large part of their time is taken up with inside repairs and maintenance of their homes and working in their garages and basement shops. Many longshoremen are do-it-yourself addicts and spend the majority of their leisure time in constructing boats, furniture, and similar items. It is doubtful whether all of these activities should be categorized as leisure activities because many contribute to the economic welfare of the family. Nonetheless, they are undertaken with the same attitudes and enjoyment as avocations that are not economically productive.

DRINKING

A form of indoor amusement indulged in by some of the longshoremen is drinking. This is usually a social affair in the home or local tavern and beer is the usual drink. Ordinarily, however, this is not carried to the point that it produces intoxication and men who indulge in social beer drinking quite frequently will claim they are not drinkers. The term "drinker" is reserved for those men who consume hard liquor on a fairly regular basis and become intoxicated on occasions but not regularly. It is not felt that going on an occasional binge is harmful and attitudes toward such men are tolerant if not approving. "Drunks," on the other hand, are persons who are at least approaching alcoholism. These are men who are often and regularly intoxicated and frequently appear on the job in that condition, and spend a large part of their income on liquor to the detriment of their family responsibilities. There are at present about twenty-five such men in the Portland longshore group, and far from being the subjects of humorous or admiring approval they are constantly criticized by the other longshoremen. A variety of drunk is the "wino," an alcoholic so far gone that he no longer works enough to be able to afford hard liquor and is reduced to slaking his thirst with cheap wine. Winos usually do not remain long on the waterfront, because of the rapid deterioration of their health and incomes.

Drinkers are fairly common among the longshoremen but do not constitute anything approaching a majority of the men. Many more of the longshoremen join the drinkers on festive occasions, and attempting to work a ship on Christmas Eve or on New Year's Eve is almost certain to produce much more intoxication than production. This has a long tradition rooted in the custom of company supervisors and general foremen supplying the longshoremen with whiskey on such occasions. I have worked on these nights several times and have seen all the longshoremen on a ship sent home early for fear that they would be killed or injured or do serious damage to the ship and cargo.

The criteria used to separate the two categories of "drinkers" and "drunks" is not really what or how much they drink or altogether whether or not they become intoxicated, but rather whether the man continues to work frequently and competently and meets his family responsibilities. Drinkers fulfill their responsibilities and drunks do not.

INTELLECTUAL AND CULTURAL ACTIVITIES

Longshoremen are not renowned for their intellectual and cultural interests. They tend to characterize themselves as men "with strong backs and weak minds." This stereotype, however, will not stand up to close scrutiny. The numbers of intellectuals in the longshore group appear to outnumber the "drunks," and seem to have no correlation with the personality traits usually associated with intellectuals. They come from within the longshore group and display much the same behavior patterns as the other men, with the one exception of having some deep and abiding intellectual interest.

There are men who attend regularly the offerings of the Civic Theatre and who appear at every showing of an opera or ballet in the city, sometimes accompanied by their wives. One man maintains an astounding collection of fine classical records and has invested a significant sum in sound equipment, but he is known to have such a bad temper that most of the men do not want to work with him. Another has made a hobby of learning foreign languages and speaks several fluently; he only works during the summer months and spends the rest of his time traveling throughout Latin America. There is at least one painter and a poet among the Portland longshoremen.

There are several men who have an interest in various phases of history and the philosophy of religion. Because of his education, the author was often used as a source of reference by some of these men. A number of the longshoremen have college degrees and more have had some college training, but the men with the deepest intellectual interests for the most part were not among the men with the highest educational achievements. To the contrary, many of the men with college training would have to be counted among those who do not engage in intellectual activity as an end in itself. One of these college-trained men is a competent mathematician who has had some work published, and there is another who aspires to be a writer.

The waterfront intellectuals appear to have two traits in common other than intellectual interests. For the most part, they do not know of the other intellectuals and do not consider themselves intellectuals. They generally lack the educational experience that would have made them self-conscious intellectuals and tend to use the word "intellectual" to mean an intellectual snob. They also appear to be less interested in acquiring material goods than do the other longshoremen. They generally drive small or inexpensive automobiles and have houses that are not as well-equipped in terms of furnishings and appliances as those of the other longshoremen.

Not every longshoreman is an Eric Hoffer, but many of them are as interested in the philosophy of life and the historical events taking place around them. I have often discussed my training and interest in anthropology with working longshoremen and many of the longshoremen were very interested in the study I was conducting among them, especially the results and conclusions. While I was conducting this study, I gave a short paper on the study at a meeting of anthropologists in Portland. I distributed no copies of this paper around the waterfront, but to my surprise within a week I discovered copies were available in the hiring hall.

9 / Work culture

When the longshoreman leaves his home and goes to his job, he enters a different world. The physical change is striking: the waterfront resembles nothing so much as a steel jungle. The apparent tangle of booms and rigging, the jumble of cargo piled on the dock, and the numbers of machines hauling cargo to and from the ship give the impression of vast confusion. Moreover, the language used to convey information concerning the work and cargo is largely incomprehensible to an outsider. This is typical of most industrial workplaces, but certain aspects of this environment are most atypical.

SKILLS

Loading a ship is a matter of placing various kinds of cargo of all different shapes and sizes into a ship having a rigid and unchangeable shape. The cargo is not designed to fit that shape and yet must be placed so that a minimum of space is lost. This problem is not improved by the fact that the cargo destined for different ports must be placed in the ship in a determined sequence so that when a particular lot of cargo is to be discharged it is not buried under a thousand tons of cargo meant to be removed in some subsequent port. The situation is never the same from one job to another and seldom the same from one hour to the next. Thus, the longshoremen's tasks are seldom boring or monotonous, although they are often hectic and exasperating.

The "tight stow"—placing cargo in the hold of the ship in such a manner that little space is left unfilled and the cargo will not shift with the heaving of the ship at sea—has long been the longshoreman's chief skill. This is not a skill that is learned in a few days but, like that of the top-hand on a cattle ranch, is learned over the course of years. The longshoremen take a great pride in this skill, and it is often said to a man who balks at a task or complains of its impossibility that "a good longshoreman can do anything." This is almost true in the sense that most of the men can perform almost any task involved in working cargo on and around the ships. The variety of these tasks and the number of small skills necessary to their performance is almost endless. Stowing sacks or canned goods would seem simple tasks and certainly are in comparison to many of the other tasks that longshoremen perform. But stowing these items so that they will not shift and fall, or so that

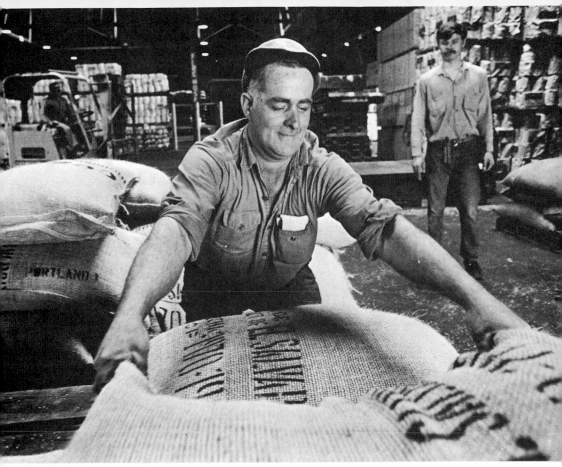

Palletizing sacks of coffee beans on the dock. (Photo by Gordon Clark)

the cases of canned goods will not chafe themselves into shreds with the vibration of the moving ship, requires the kind of knowledge that comes only with long experience.

The skill spectrum has shifted a great deal in recent years. More and more operating skills are needed and less and less of the older longshoremen's skills: that is, manual work techniques necessary to obtaining a tight stow and moving very large and heavy pieces of cargo. In addition to knowing these "tricks of the trade" for handling cargo in the hold of the ship or on the docks, longshoremen are expected to be able to operate a growing number of ever more complex hauling and hoisting equipment. A majority of men can operate many kinds of sizes of lift machines and many types of winches and cranes. Some men can operate nearly all of these machines.

OUTSIDERS IN THE WORKPLACE

The longshoremen are very possessive in their attitudes toward their workplace. Sailors, other dock and ship personnel, and ship repair crews are the only other categories of people that belong in the workplace. These workers are treated in very much the same manner as longshoremen, but outsiders, such as stevedore company administrative personnel, are regarded as interlopers and often treated very rudely. The wearing of a suit and tie is the mark of an outsider and makes the person wearing them fair game for all sorts of practical jokes. One young man whose job was to check the amount of carbon monoxide in the air in the cargo hatches where machines were being used was left standing around on the deck of a ship for some time because no one, including the general foreman from the same company, would tell him how to enter the hatch. Many other forms of misdirection or nondirection of such persons are common, while men dressed in work clothes are generally treated in a helpful manner. Another sort of joke played on men wearing business suits by the winch drivers is to attempt to "drop the fall on him." This means operating the winch in such a manner that the victim will be struck by the slack portion of the wire rope used as a winch fall or runner. This wire is nearly always covered with extremely heavy, sticky grease and will so thoroughly stain a piece of cloth that expert professional cleaning is required to remove it.

WORK SOCIALIZATION

Longshoremen have a great deal of opportunity for socializing with one another in the work context because of the uneven pace of the work and the fact that they work in teams, called "gangs." Delays in getting cargo to and from the ship are common, which gives the longshoremen ample time to visit and gossip, one of their favorite pastimes. Not only do the longshoremen have plentiful opportunity to socialize with one another and thus cement relations with other members of the group, but these informal "caucuses" keep them well informed of current happenings around the waterfront. Information about members of the group who are not present is exchanged among all of the men working on the job, and all of their virtues and faults are given ample consideration and are well-expounded. It is in this context that newcomers to the waterfront learn what forms of behavior are expected from them: from the criticism levelled against absent members of the longshore group as well as from the praise they may receive.

In this way new men are thoroughly indoctrinated by the older union men in approved union principles and work strategies, and it is apparent that they learn swiftly from this kind of instruction. The incentive to accept this indoctrination derives from the way in which B men gain A status (see pages 65–66). The A men form the group (the union membership) that makes the final decision as to whether or not any particular B man will be promoted to A status.

ENFORCEMENT OF NORMS

Among themselves and with other persons that they feel belong in the workplace the longshoremen maintain friendly and extremely informal relations. They resent any attempt on the part of a foreman or ship's officer to express social distance. Such an attitude will always elicit hostility on the part of the longshoremen. This hostility will invariably result in an attempt to "bring him down a few notches." The methods used to put an offender in his place vary with the person and the situation, but the method used to humble foremen is about the same at all times. Often the foreman will be "told off," in rather harsh terms, but this is not the end of the retaliation. The most effective and most common method, is to institute the "slowdown" in an attempt to make the foreman's work record look bad to the company. This method is also used when a foreman "chisels" the men out of time or mistreats the longshoremen in other ways. One foreman who was a constant offender became so consistently the target for the "slowdown" that he could obtain no employment with a stevedore company for months and was forced to fall back on unemployment compensation. Few foremen ever attempt to assume any role other than that of "one of the boys," and those who maintain themselves as part of the longshore in-group enjoy a good deal of popularity among the men and maintain good production records, because the longshoremen will usually give a break to a foreman who maintains his status as one of the men.

Conformity to group norms is obtained within the group of longshoremen in much the same manner as it is among foremen. The foremost offense that one longshoreman can deliver to another is to shirk his share of the work so that more work is shifted onto the other members of the work crew. Various techniques are used, from offering to fight to simply sitting down and making the offender do all of the work for a time. The most common method, however is to shift more work onto the victim by various means or by refusing to do more than their share of the work so that the offender comes to the attention of the foreman. "Finking" on a nonconforming longshoreman by telling the foreman of his misbehavior is not an approved form of obtaining conformity and, in fact, is considered a worse offense than not doing one's fair share of the work.

Another technique used to discipline a longshoreman who thus abuses his fellows is to embarrass him by showing up his misbehavior to the entire work crew and subjecting him to the ridicule of the entire longshore group. Longshoremen like to think of themselves as hard workers, and the reputation of being a loafer is not a happy one. In one incident, a cargo gang was stowing "Jap squares," huge timbers measuring two to four feet square. To turn one of these timbers with peaveys required the combined efforts of the entire hold crew of eight men. One man was suspected of just "going through the motions" and making each of the other longshoremen expend additional energy to make up for his lack of effort. During the lunch break, the steel bolt that holds the cant hook onto the shaft was removed from the loafer's peavey, and a piece of soft wood was carved to the proper size and inserted in place of the bolt. The offender worked for two hours with the peavey and was exposed when one of the other men took the peavey and easily broke off the wooden pin by prying on the next timber to be stowed. This story was told for a considerable length of time in every longshore "bull session," and the offender is still reminded of his "wooden bolt" some ten years after the incident took place.

PILFERING

Pilfering of cargo is common to every waterfront in the world, and Portland is no exception, although the Portland longshoremen do not carry this activity to the extent of hauling away truckloads of cargo, as in some of the Eastern Ports. Generally they confine themselves to small objects that will fit in a pocket or inside their shirts or jackets without causing a noticeable bulge. Cargo is seldom stolen for sale, but rather for consumption or use by the longshoremen, their families, and friends. Most longshoremen do not consider pilfering cargo stealing, and men who are otherwise scrupulously honest will happily fill their pockets with whiskey or small merchandise. Few of the longshoremen would consider stealing from an individual, but a large company or corporation is not a person, and it seems to them that a few small items from a shipment that may exceed a thousand tons is not likely to cause deprivation to anyone. Baggage and other personal belongings are usually not pilfered, and the personal belongings of other longshoremen and the ship's crew are ordinarily quite safe from theft by longshoremen.

Stealing a worker's tools is thought to be the most reprehensible sort of misbehavior because like most workers, longshoremen regard a man's tools as his means for earning a living. On one occasion I witnessed, a carpenter's tools were stolen on a Dutch ship, apparently by a longshoreman. Rather than closing ranks and refusing even to discuss the matter as they normally do when one of them is accused of theft, all of the longshoremen aboard joined the carpenter in an attempt to find and recover his tools.

Liquor, transistor radios, and other relatively small and desirable objects are always subject to pilfering, and the longshoremen are more than ingenious in obtaining them. Moreover shipping companies have not always shown a great concern for the security of the cargo in their ships. More recently, however, competition has greatly increased the zeal with which these companies protect their cargo, bringing them into direct conflict with the established habits of the longshoremen. One of the more successful precautions employed to discourage the extensive pilfering of liquor was the practice of ships' mates of opening a case of liquor and distributing it to the longshoremen in the gang. This was fairly successful because the longshoremen felt that it was not really proper to steal from such a congenial fellow and the degree of intoxication produced made it much easier for the mate to observe their activities and stop any attempts to pilfer the cargo. More liquor was usually lost when the mate attempted to keep the longshoremen from getting any of it than when a small amount was distributed.

On one occasion, when a gang of longshoremen were discharging whiskey, under the watchful eyes of a mate who insisted that they were not going to steal any of the whiskey, it appeared that the longshoremen might fail in their attempts to steal it. However, when the last slingloads of whiskey were being loaded, the mate turned his back to one of the longshoremen just long enough for him to slip several pints under a piece of waterproof paper. Knowing that the mate would search the hatch before leaving, one of the longshoremen unzipped his fly and urinated on the paper. The mate did search the hatch, but the one place he did not look was under the waterproof paper. The urine, of course, had never touched the bottles.

Another method used to steal pure alcohol is also interesting in its ingenuity. The alcohol was shipped in steel drums which the shipping company obviously believed impervious to pilferage. This did present an obstacle to the longshoremen but not an insurmountable one. They waited until the alcohol was buried under six feet of other cargo, and then, one of the longshoremen, carrying a hammer and a two-by-four into which a large spike had been driven, slid down between the internal ribs of the ship. He drove the spike through the two by four and into the side of the steel drum a few inches from the top and then filled various containers that the other men passed down to him. When the hole in the barrel no longer gave forth alcohol, the spike was driven into the barrel a few inches below the original hole. One man, feeling limited by the size of container he could carry on his person, worked out a method for carrying a gallon at a time. He used clear half gallon jugs which he filled to the very top so that there would be no visible bubble of air at the neck and simply walked out of the dock with the apparently empty jugs in plain sight of the guards on the dock.

The tradition of pilfering is so well established that many longshoremen feel that they have a right to pilfer and resent attempts to stop them as unjust. That this is well recognized by the longshoremen themselves is evidenced by the actions of a longshoreman who shipped his personal automobile from Hawaii to the West Coast: he placed a note inside the windshield stating that the auto belonged to a longshoreman and member of the ILWU. The car was handled with special care and nothing was stolen from it. One longshoreman in the gang unloading the auto stated that this man "certainly knew his brothers."

It must, however, be stressed that pilfering is strictly part of longshore work behavior. There are out-and-out thieves among the longshoremen, and most of the men know who they are and do not trust them, but well-known "cargo inspectors" are often scrupulously honest in all other ways.

10 / Joking behavior

There is a considerable literature dealing with the "colorful language" of roughneck workers, most of which does not begin to treat the subject in a serious or scientific manner. Often such treatises only deal with the "quaint" boasts and brags of frontiersmen and the few serious works are compilations of occupational jargons. The profanity used by such workers has been either ignored, on the grounds that such utterances are merely the products of ignorance and crudity of background and are, therefore, meaningless, or sadly misinterpreted. This is more an example of middle class ethnocentricity than anything else, for although the meanings of human utterances are sometimes opaque, they are seldom empty of significance. The profanity so frequently used by longshoremen is neither meaningless nor without useful functions for both the group and individuals. Rather, a great part of it constitutes what has been called joking behavior. This term, first used by Radcliffe-Brown (1952) is something of a misnomer, for it refers to a kind of ceremonially licensed behavior in which insults are exchanged between persons occupying particular and well-defined statuses within some social structure. The insults exchanged are such that in any other context they would express and elicit hostility, but which within the appropriate social contexts express and elicit not hostility or conflict, but rather personal friendliness and solidarity. Such behavior is not optional for those persons occupying the statuses that share a joking relationship, but is ordinarily mandatory. The relationship marked by joking behavior is called a joking relationship, and is always a primary rather than a secondary relationship.

PROFANITY

Joking behavior as defined by Radcliffe-Brown (1952) has not been reported for American workers. Perhaps a major reason for the lack of such observations is the widespread use of profanity by nearly all workers and indeed by nearly all males when in purely male contexts, and this has most certainly been abetted by the general taboo on the use of profanity in "polite" company (in the presence of women). Also, the attitude that the use of "dirty words" and vulgar language can be of no scientific interest because it is simply the result of bad manners and a lack of education has aggravated matters.

Indeed, so deeply embedded is the taboo on the use of obscene Anglo-Saxon that one seeks in vain for examples of the obscenities used specially in articles dealing with English speaking groups, a regrettable tendency that will not be followed here.

The pattern of joking behavior among longshoremen is, again, not easy to detect because of the "smokescreen" of profanity that is normally present whenever they are working. This profanity falls into three major categories, each with its own set of context restrictions and functions.

1. Blasphemy
2. Cursing and references to ancestry
3. Obscenity

Blasphemy is a highly developed art among longshoremen. Exclamations such as "jumping H. Jesus Blue Christ," "Christ on a sawed-off goddam crutch," and many similarly ingenious forms of blasphemy are common on the waterfront. One of the favorite pastimes of many longshoremen is inventing new and ever more color-ful forms. The use of this blasphemy is never random, but like all other forms of waterfront profanity is highly patterned in its use. Although such blasphemy is commonly used as an exclamation of surprise, or bewilderment, its chief use is to give vent to frustration: it plays a major part in the release of psychological tension produced by the work or the work environment.

Cursing and references to ancestry, although constantly to be heard where long-shoremen are working are almost never directed at longshoremen. Rather, they are used in much the same way toward inanimate objects, the cargo, the ship, tools, the company, and company representatives who are not members of the longshore group. Men will often be heard to utter such phrases as "Goddam this dirty, son of a bitchin' ship" or to refer to a tool, such as a peavey, as a "dirty son of a bitch." Nearly all winches and other machines are described by the adjectives "goddam, bastardly, or motherless," and these again are usually interspersed with obsceni-ties such as "fucking" and often accompanied by blasphemous oaths.

Obscenity in its purer forms is used in several ways. No statement is quite com-plete without at least one obscene term, most often simply "fuck" or some com-pound thereof. It is obscenity primarily in the form of obscene Anglo–Saxon compounds referring to sexual and excretory functions that forms the basic vocab-ulary of longshore joking behavior and which is often mistaken for expressions of hostility and aggression by outsiders. It is important to note here that the obscen-ity longshoremen address to one another seldom expresses hostility or constitutes aggression but rather connotes friendship, affection, and warm personal feeling. This point cannot be overstressed: the mutual vituperation of the working long-shoremen expresses exactly the opposite of its overt meaning. When one longshore-man calls another a "dirty cocksucker, a shiteating asshole" or addresses him by any other obscene term or combination of terms, he is expressing affection and reaffirming a deeply felt personal regard. It clearly marks a significant primary relationship: a joking relationship. If any of the longshoremen thought that such remarks were seriously meant, the only possible outcome would be violence. Vio-lence is, however, extremely rare among the longshoremen.

The profanity used by working longshoremen serves several functions in its totality and in its parts. Profanity serves, primarily, to reinforce and reaffirm the "rough-and-tough" image that the longshoremen like to project to one another and to outsiders. Blasphemy is primarily a device for relieving pent up tensions deriving from the frustrations of the work. Cursing, both in the more common forms and in the form concerned with the ancestry of inanimate objects and the stevedore and steamship companies, serves to release hostility resulting from the hazards and other perversities of the work and the work situation. The use of obscenities serves to minimize the chances of physical conflict, to reaffirm personal relationships, and to mark the boundaries of the longshore group.

SPEECH CONTEXTS

The use of profanity and especially the obscenity that forms the core of long-shore joking behavior is restricted by the physical and social environment in which the longshoremen, find themselves. Like most other Americans, the longshoremen do not ordinarily use any form of profanity in the presence of women, although they may use it extensively at other times. Moreover, the different forms of profanity are felt to be appropriate only in specific and highly restricted contexts: as the longshoremen move from one sphere of activity to another, their verbal behavior undergoes several transformations.

THE FEMININE CONTEXT

In any context where women may be present the use of profanity is absolutely forbidden. Longshoremen, like most American men, consider the use of profanity in the presence of women offensive, but unlike many others, nearly all longshore-men consider violation of this norm ample reason to fight. In fact, many if not all of the longshoremen consider this to be such an offense that they will react to "defend" a woman without discovering whether she wishes to be defended. I have witnessed several such cases, and the presence of women in the longshore hiring hall is discouraged because of past incidents in which persons were seriously injured. Usually, such incidents involved a longshoreman who violated the taboo when intoxicated, a risk arising from the location of a bar across the street from the hiring hall. The greatest offense, however, is not simply the use of profanity, and a simple blasphemy or curse may occur without more than passing notice and elicit little more than a frown or a command to cease. On the other hand, the use of obscenity in such circumstances is almost certain to produce violence. Joking behav-ior in its various forms is completely absent in this context, except some very mild forms that will be described later.

THE INGROUP CONTEXT

It is only within the ingroup context that the verbal forms of longshore joking behavior appear, for any other context is potentially feminine. The first of several forms of speech behavior to manifest itself when the longshoremen enter the hiring hall or any other ingroup context is the use of derogatory nicknames. These names are loaded with emotion. Although they are unlike many of the other linguistic devices of longshore profanity in that they are often not Anglo-Saxon in derivation, they are frequently marked by Anglo-Saxon or Germanic compounding. That is, a compound will display the normal stress pattern of a polysyllabic Germanic word: the stress will fall on the first part of the compound, as in "bóarhog," which clearly marks them as unitary terms.

Their nicknames are probably the most colorful part of the entire linguistic repertoire of the longshoremen, and are nearly always insulting, although their derogatory nature is not always apparent to outsiders. Some of the nicknames commonly used by longshoremen are Mule-shoes, Horse-thief, Longdong, Cesspool, Saddle-tramp, Burglar, Gangster, Snake, Whip, Jowls, Wino, Bignose, and Professor. These nicknames are not assigned in a random fashion. They are usually descriptive of the individual's physiognomy (Bignose), derived from some distinguishing activity (Burglar, Cesspool, Professor), or are a pun made on the man's real name (Shanghai, the word "China" is embedded in this individual's surname). Occasionally, they are related to the man's ethnic background (the Mad Russian) or to his religious affiliation (Pope, Preacher, Jew).

Nicknames are seldom given to persons who are not generally well liked. It should be stressed that these names would not be used if the recipients truly objected to their use for they would evoke too much violence. I know of two occasions when attempts to nickname men with names that they found truly offensive were abandoned as soon as it became clear that they were really angered by the use of the proposed nicknames.

These names are properly used only within the longshore ingroup: it is considered inappropriate to use a man's nickname in any other context. It is a *faux pas* to use a man's nickname outside of the ingroup context, but in the absence of women it is only a *faux pas* and not a serious offense. In the presence of women, however, the use of a nickname usually produces an angry retort, and in the presence of female members of the man's family may be productive of violence. In one instance, a man's nickname was used in the presence of his wife by one of his best friends to which he replied by battering the offender into insensibility, and this extremely violent response was not felt to be excessive by either the other longshoremen or the victim of the attack.

THE WORKPLACE: MUTUAL VITUPERATION

As the longshoremen move further away from the feminine context and approach the uniquely masculine world of work, their use of the crudest profanity becomes more and more extensive. It increases even more as they move onto the job, especially as they go aboard the ships. As previously mentioned, all three types of profanity are in constant use, but by far the most notable linguistic device used (in this context) is the Anglo-Saxon compound noun. The ingroup nicknames are used freely and extensively and often in sentences composed almost entirely

Loading barrels of scrap metal. (Photo by Gordon Clark)

of powerful combinations of normally taboo words and phrases. These utterances
are pronounced in a manner that can only be described as joyful as men arrive on
the job. There are two phases of this activity, each phase serving somewhat different functions.

As men arrive on the docks before the work begins, they congregate in the dock
lunchroom or on the apron of the dock in good weather. Here they begin to insult
one another very severely; the scene is reminiscent of athletes warming up before
a game. One man may begin by insulting the entire group of longshoremen present,
who then return the insults in more aggravated forms, and much sport is had in
attempting to outdo the vile insults received. Combined with the verbal assault,
there is often what appears to be a physical assault. This does not consist of a
simple, friendly pat on the shoulder or a playful approach, but rather of a realistic fighting approach accompanied by much vilification. Usually this terminates
in a rough scuffle involving a great deal of bodily contact and exertion. Outsiders,
observing these proceedings have been known to become alarmed and try to stop
the "fight." I have observed occasions when a beginning longshoreman thought
he was actually being attacked and tried to defend himself before he discovered
that the attack was a sham. To the longshoremen this is clearly a game and they
derive a good deal of enjoyment from it, but the foremost rule of the game is that
it must appear serious.

The principal function of this prework warm-up is to reaffirm group solidarity
and identification. There is no element of hostility and it would, therefore, be a
serious error to describe this behavior as aggression. Outsiders are expected to take
no part in these games, and in fact, it would be physically dangerous to do so.
New longshoremen are not expected to initiate this sort of behavior, until established
group members have signified their acceptance of the newcomers into the group
by vilifying them in the same manner as they would other established members.
This activity is, among other things, a symbol of group membership, and any attempt to fraudulently display the symbols of membership receives about the same
degree of welcome that it does in any other group. It will be observed that some
men never insult one another and that others insult one another continuously, because those men who truly dislike one another do not engage in joking behavior
with one another, while those who are close friends tend to do so more often than
others. In other words, where hostility is present, mutual vituperation is normally
absent.

After the men begin work, the behavior begun in the pre-work period changes
in tone. Although the shift is slight among those men who perform their tasks on
the dock, there is a very clear change aboard the ships. All forms of profanity become more frequent and more serious in tone. The insults are more often directed
toward individuals, are more serious in nature, and the mock assaults although less
frequent are more realistic than ever. While the tone of the banter becomes lighter
on the docks, and is often clearly playful even to outsiders, it becomes more serious
on the ships. Again, outsiders often mistake the insults and horseplay on the ships
for real hostility and aggression.

Generally, the presence of outsiders in the work environment has no effect
on the verbal behavior of the longshoremen; however, one class of nonlongshore-

Single winch driver at work. Note the tangle of machinery and rigging and the high deck load of lumber, all of which contributes to the hazard of the job. (Photo by Gordon Clark)

men do affect this behavior, the longshoremen's families. Longshoremen often bring their families onto the waterfront to show them where and how they work. On such an occasion, notice of their imminent approach is passed along the dock and onto the ship, and all profanity ceases until the visiting family has passed out of range of the longshoremen's voices. Classes of visiting school children are handled in the same manner, but other persons may well expect to have their linguistic sensibilities offended if they persist in spending too much time around the working longshoremen.

Much of the behavior described above is not unusual for American males in general. Throughout our society, it is quite common for men to symbolize their affection for one another by means of slightly derogatory nicknames and manners of address, and most American males tend to use strong Anglo-Saxon when in purely male company. However, there are certain systematic differences between this usage and that of longshoremen. First, there is the matter of degree and frequency. From my own rather wide experience with other groups, industrial and otherwise, it seems clear that the terms and forms of address used by the Portland longshoremen are rather distinctive. Only in the armed forces and among loggers have I ever encountered the use of such deeply derogatory nicknames and forms of address. Nor have I ever encountered such a consistent and frequent use of taboo Anglo-Saxon terms other than in these contexts.

CAUSES OF JOKING BEHAVIOR

Of the forms of behavior described, linguistic and otherwise, the least important is the extensive use of profanity. The complex of derogatory nicknames, insults formed around Anglo-Saxon obscene words, and pretended but very realistic physical assault is the core phenomenon. This behavior centers around the workplace, and would not be acceptable if seriously intended or in any other place. As the longshoremen leave the job, most of this behavior is abandoned. In union meetings, it is generally absent, and the Anglo-Saxon terms are reserved for the expression of strongly held beliefs and for underscoring points in arguments. The ingroup nicknames are sometimes used in meetings as they are in other ingroup situations, but forms of address garnished with Anglo-Saxon compound nouns are not to be heard. Longshoremen, encountering one another in public places often engage in an extremely abbreviated and clearly playful form of the more violent scuffle that takes place on the job as a sign of recognition of an ingroup member. The extreme forms of this behavior stand in stark contrast to that of white-collar workers. Their world of work lies in a feminine sphere: there are nearly always women in their workplace. As the male white-collar worker approaches his place of employment, his use of Anglo-Saxon decreases, which is quite contrary to the longshoreman's behavior. Moreover, white-collar workers do not engage in the liberal use of derogatory nicknames and crude Anglo-Saxon comments about their fellow workers as they come onto the job. They are much more likely to indulge in such behavior in the context of a lodge, club, or some other informal masculine gathering.

The mere absence of women in the work place does not, however, seem to be a sufficient explanation for the longshoreman's work behavior, for many other workers in similar female-free environs do not display this complex of behavior. Lack of education and general crudity of background offer no better explanation, for other blue-collar workers with similar backgrounds do not display this behavior complex.

NATURE OF THE WORKPLACE

An examination of the longshore workplace and the conditions under which longshoremen work is enlightening. There is a general distinction between the ship and the dock. Much less of the behavior described takes place when long-shoremen are working on the dock than when the same men are working on board ships, and what does occur is much milder in tone. It is also possible to distinguish between the kinds of work performed on the ships. On ships where logs or long steel beams and plates are being handled, or where the work is especially arduous, seemingly bitter mutual verbal abuse is almost constant, and mock assaults are very frequent. On other shipboard operations, this behavior is not serious in appearance and clearly conveys a sense of easygoing good fellowship as it does among the men working on the docks.

There are two factors involved here. Commodities such as logs and long steel are extremely dangerous cargoes to handle. When a cargo of this type is being

Longshoremen at the dispatch window. Information about jobs being hired is on the small blackboard at upper left. (Photo by Gordon Clark)

worked, all of the longshoremen are extremely tense, and they are easily angered. The same is true of men who are performing very strenuous labor. They become tense as soon as they approach the ship and discover that the cargo they will be working is hazardous or involves very hard work, which is clearly expressed by the tense and alert postures they assume as they approach the gangplank. This is almost never true of the longshoremen working on the pier.

Longshoremen and probably many other workers work under conditions that create nervous strain. This, in turn, often leads to anger. Most of us are familiar with the experience of feeling quick and often irrational anger when interrupted while working and tense. Unlike many other people, however, longshoremen often become aggressive and sometimes violent when angered. Because longshoremen tend to come from backgrounds in which physical violence is often seen as a legitimate means for the settlement of certain kinds of disputes, many of them are not only willing to fight without extreme provocation but are also comparatively skilled fist-fighters.

DANGER AND THE PRODUCTION OF TENSION

The longshore work place is already fraught with dangers which conflict can only aggravate. A man working aboard a ship must be constantly alert if he is not to be injured. The shipboard environment is a veritable jungle of rigging used to hoist heavy loads of cargo on and off the ship. These loads must be avoided and care must be exercised not to trip over the wires and rigging on deck or to fall over the side or into one of the the open cargo holds. Negligence concerning these precautions often produces serious and sometimes fatal injuries. A longshoreman must try to be conscious of his total environment while working aboard a ship. He must be aware of what is happening above him and on all sides, and must also be careful of where he steps. Clearly, he cannot maintain essential caution while engaging in a fight. Moreover, if he were to be knocked down, he could easily fall into the river or an open hatch, become entangled in the gears or other moving parts of the hoisting machinery, or suffer a serious injury by simply falling on the steel deck. Aggression and violence in the longshoremen's work place must be controlled in order to avoid these consequences.

CONTROL OF AGGRESSION

Some means are obviously needed to control overt aggression: first, a means of tension release, of relieving pent-up emotions; and second, a method of minimizing the probability that this will result in uncontrolled aggression. Both of these needs can be met by the granting of certain kinds of license in the work context. The use of vile expletives is a common means of emotional release in all segments of modern American society as it is in many others. Most of us have verbally vented our frustrations over the refusal of some inanimate object to perform its given function, and striking oneself on the thumb with a hammer is normally accepted as an occasion to exercise one's full command of Anglo-Saxon obscenities and blasphemous oaths.

Longshoremen normally tend to be rather touchy concerning the manner in which they are addressed. I have seen a general foreman forced to flee from the ship in order to avoid being assaulted by a pugnacious longshoreman who objected to the manner in which the foreman had spoken to him. I have also witnessed several fights that began because some outsider had made a comment about the sexual habits of a longshoreman in much milder terms than the longshoremen normally use among themselves. In the work context, the perversity that longshoremen find the most occasion to bemoan is some act of one of their own number. Yet, it clearly would not do for a longshoreman to give vent to his feelings in such a situation without some means of preventing physical conflict. This is provided by allowing him to address his fellows in the most uncomplimentary of terms whenever he is working and, on occasion, when off the job but in the context of the ingroup. This creates a climate in which it is extremely easy to pass off or mistake some rash statement as merely a part of the usual banter. I have seen several cases when one longshoreman had lost his temper and challenged another to fight, but the challenge went unrecognized until the aggrieved party was no longer angry.

This license, however, has very clear limits. Rarely is a longshoreman heard to direct a blasphemous statement to one of his fellow workers or to curse him. Even more rarely do they refer to another longshoreman's ancestry or make any statement that might be construed to imply that the man was ever a strikebreaker or company informer. Consequently, the terms "scab" and "fink" are almost never used in reference to any other longshoreman. No disparaging remarks concerning another longshoreman's family or close friends are made except in very circumscribed situations. Any violation of these clearly delineated boundaries would almost certainly lead to very real hostility and aggression. Such incidents do, of course, occur, but they are rare in the extreme.

FUNCTIONS OF JOKING BEHAVIOR

According to the criteria set forth by Radcliffe-Brown (1952), it is abundantly clear that the phenomena described constitute a classic form of joking behavior. The use of the derogatory nicknames and insults acceptable in the work context would most certainly "express and arouse hostility" in any other social situation. The limits beyond which one may not go without incurring the wrath of one's fellows are clearly set by custom, and one may not take offense at the abuse heaped upon him so long as it remains within these limits. There are, however, certain problems involved in reconciling my data with Radcliffe-Brown's description of joking behavior and the joking relationship.

Although the waterfront form of joking behavior fits neatly in Radcliffe-Brown's thesis that the foremost function of joking behavior is to control and prevent aggression in order that a stable system of social behavior may be maintained, it also serves as an important boundary and symbol of group solidarity for the longshore ingroup and probably contributes to some unknown degree to the maintenance of this solidarity. This function of joking behavior was to some degree recognized by Radcliffe-Brown when he stated that the joking relationship is a relation of alliance (Radcliffe-Brown 1952). The persons sharing a joking relationship, whether it exists primarily between tribes, clans, or lineages, clearly form a special and socially significant group, and joking behavior undoubtedly serves as a symbol of group membership and solidarity for these non-Western groups as much as it does for the longshoremen. However, the concepts of the joking relationship and joking behavior must be broadened if they are to have any explanatory power in the longshore case, because longshore joking behavior is in no way connected with kinship or the alliance of disparate and normally hostile groups.

The source of tension in the longshore case does not spring from the association of members of corporate groups who ordinarily share only a mutual antipathy, but rather from the irritations of performing arduous labor and/or working in a hazardous place. It is individuals *as* individuals that must accommodate one another and not persons as members of divergently oriented groups. While Radcliffe-Brown has consistently stressed the importance of intragroup and affinal relations as the source of joking behavior, these factors appear to be of no significance to an explanation of longshore joking behavior.

11 / Summary, prospectus, and conclusions

COMMUNITY INSTITUTIONS

Any internal urban community must have a set of community institutions around which it is focused and which impart continuity to the social organization of the group. In the Portland longshoremen's case, the core around which the community is organized consists primarily of the union, reinforced by widely ramified kinship networks. The union is the basic institution since it regulates the hiring and the work and transmits a sense of identity to all of its members. The union provides the structure in which members may gain prestige in the eyes of their peers, seek individual fulfillment by serving as union officials, and serves as a center for the communication network that spreads throughout the longshore group.

The longshoremen are not hired by company representatives nor do they consistently accept employment from certain stevedore companies, rather they are dispatched from a union operated hiring hall on a rotating basis. The only role played by employer representatives consists of placing the work orders, since the dispatchers are quasi officials of the union. Which longshoremen will fill a work order is determined almost solely by chance, depending on who happens to be in the hiring hall on that day, which longshoremen are first or last to be hired, and on whether that particular job is considered a good or a bad choice among all those available at that time. Thus, the longshoremen regard the union as the source of employment rather than individual companies or the Pacific Maritime Association (Philpott n.d.).

The hiring system also has the effect of bringing all the longshoremen together in the hiring hall in an entirely random manner. Each longshoreman will at some time be in the hiring hall with every other longshoreman in the port and will undoubtedly have occasion to engage in sociable conversation, play cards, or have coffee or beer with every other longshoreman in the period after the plugs have been placed in the box and the actual hiring. After the hiring, many of the men who have not secured employment for the day hang around the hall on the chance that a late job will be hired after the regular hiring period, thus creating another opportunity for social contact with other longshoremen. Moreover, the random manner in which men are dispatched to their jobs insures that each longshoreman will sooner or later work closely with every other longshoreman in the port, and again there is plenty of opportunity for social contact on the job since longshore-men work in teams and few of the longshoremen like working in isolation from their fellows. For those reasons, every longshoreman in the port has at least some passing acquaintance with every other longshoreman and more highly developed ties with many others, a situation very unlike that of many blue-collar workers who are effectively isolated from most of their fellows during the work day and have little opportunity or reason to develop social contacts at other times.

This effect is again heightened by the necessity to take part in the operation of the union. All union members are required to attend monthly meetings, and to vote in all elections. Such activities are enforced by the application of fines for a first failure to participate and by removal from the work list for repeated offenses. It cannot be too strongly stressed that this local is actively operated by its member-ship. The union rules upon which these penalties are based were formulated by the executive board of the union and ratified by the membership as a body. More-over, active participation in the political processes of the union is very much en-couraged by the political structure of the union.

Thus, the union serves as the center and focus of the community, welding the longshoremen together into a social group and furnishing them with a very real community of interest, since it is their participation in the operation of the union that determines the way they are hired, the conditions under which they work, and forges the union into an effective collective bargaining agent.

Another set of institutions binding the longshore community together are the legends and myths surrounding the founding of the present union local in 1934. The 1934 strike produced a great change, not only in the working conditions and hiring procedures of the Portland waterfront, but also in the nature of the group and their way of life. Before the strike, the Portland longshoremen had never formed a cohesive social group, but the strike itself brought them together in a common endeavor of great magnitude and importance in their lives.

The effect of the strike on the longshoremen was very similar to that of a suc-cessful revolutionary war on a people: it gave a sense of having engaged in impor-tant historical processes and working together toward a common goal. There was a fair amount of actual physical violence during the strike and the tales of the battles fought are passed on from generation to generation of longshoremen. The battles grow somewhat more important and more magnificent in each telling, and the principal figures in some of these have almost the stature of George Washing-ton and John Paul Jones. Indeed, all of these legends have become welded together into one great origin myth. In the beginning the employer ruled supreme and all longshoremen were little more than slaves, but under the leadership of Harry Bridges the nobler of the longshoremen arose in righteous wrath, demolished the power of the employer, and delivered their fellow workers from onerous servitude and humiliation. There is a good deal of simple truth behind this myth. Working conditions on the Portland waterfront prior to 1934 were brutal, the lives of the longshoremen were financially precarious, men were blackballed from the water-front for any kind of union activity, loan sharks flourished, and employer hiring practices were characterized by injustice and corruption.

The men who actually participated in the 1934 strike ("'34 men") have until recently, when their numbers were depleted by retirement and death, formed the core of the Local. They passed on most of the legends and stood as examples for the younger longshoremen. Among the " '34 men," however, by far the most important were the more distinguished members of the riot squads, who offered living testimonial to the fact that the battles had been fought and won. The legends of the group center around these heroic figures whose battles and exploits are recounted in the hiring halls and lunchrooms almost every day. Indeed, a special deference is shown to these now grizzled warriors, and special privileges have been granted to some of them. The Bloody Thursday ritual also serves to tie the generations together and to point out in dramatic form the central role of the union and group solidarity in maintaining the community's way of life.

LONGSHORE SUBCULTURE

The subculture of the Portland longshore group probably bears a greater resemblance to that of other Oregonians than to any other class of people in the country. Oregon forms a sort of cultural enclave even within the context of the Northwest due to its pattern of immigration, low population, and industrial structure; and the longshoremen would seem to form yet another enclave within the state-wide enclave. The longshoremen share many of the features of the "stable working class" (Miller and Riessman 1964), but there are several differences in the accent placed on some features, and others lie completely outside the purvey of this class.

The extreme accent placed on physical courage and strength would seem unusual for an ordinary working class group, although it is not too dissimilar from that of the miners described by Gouldner (1954). This value on courage as well as the willingness to engage in physical aggression is probably related to the day-to-day need to face a good deal of physical danger in the workplace. It could be accounted for as a sort of survival of the frontier period; but there are men in the group who are relatively recent migrants from the East and Midwest, and they display the same values and behavior.

The occupational genealogies of the longshoremen are not what one would expect from blue-collar workers. If the longshoremen, loggers, and farmers are deleted from the list there are for the most part only businessmen, professionals, semiprofessionals, and skilled workers. There are certain important similarities between these occupations: they involve certain sets of skills that are highly transferable. The persons having these skills are not obliged to live in one particular location or maintain an affiliation with any one business firm in order to earn a livelihood. To the contrary, such persons tend to be highly mobile. Another feature of the occupational histories of the longshore families is that they tend to present mirror images between the grandparent and grandchild generations. Again, this is only true if farmers are not included. This would seem to indicate a great deal of occupational mobility within certain specific types of occupations over time.

The depth of family involvement, making hunting and fishing trips into family affairs, and the very real stability of the longshoremen's families again seems unusual. This is very likely a reflection of the lack of some of the strains of typical blue-collar life deriving from the fear of the lay-off and deep financial problems rather than an intrinsic characteristic of the group. Another factor that contributes, to some unknown degree, to a stable family life is the great stability of residence and occupation. Most of the longshore families have deep local roots and few members of the longshore group ever leave the area or the industry for any length of time. Thus, kin networks are more extensive than they would otherwise be, and this again contributes to the stability of the group and the ability to engage in family affairs.

The deep value placed on individualism, personal independence, and freedom from a rigid work regime is one of the most striking features of the group. It is doubtful that this value has any relationship to any factors other than the old line American and Scandinavian ancestry of the overwhelming majority of the longshoremen, and that none of these men or their immediate ancestors have ever found it necessary to submit to the rigid way of life imposed by machine production and the assembly line. They are very aware that other workers must submit to these abhorrent conditions, but rather than feeling sympathy toward these workers, the longshoremen are much more likely to express contempt.

The extra-work economic activities of the longshoremen again do not fit within the framework of the "stable working class" subculture. Although the nature of this set of activities is quite different from that of other workers, the motivation for such economic strivings is even more at variance with the blue-collar norm. The agricultural portion of the economic activities of the group is not especially noteworthy since this seems to be common to the entire Northwest. Many of their other economic activities are also related to the nature of the area and its regional subculture. The motivation for engaging in extra-work economic activities may also be to some degree due to regional factors, but there is little doubt that it also differs sharply from the motivation of most blue-collar workers. The motivation is quite simply to contribute to the economic welfare of the longshoreman and his family, although there are a few men who seem totally engrossed in acquiring wealth as an end in itself. There is no concern with gaining social status or prestige, which is the usual reported motivation for blue-collar businessmen. But this may well be a false dichotomy, because the longshoremen tend to be native Americans and nearly all of the reported cases of blue-collar workers seeking social status have dealt with groups of recent immigrant backgrounds, and immigrants are nearly always more concerned with social mobility than are native Americans.

The longshoremen's attitudes toward race are unusual for any reported group of workers in that they are not deeply concerned with race *per se*. Only Negroes have been excluded from the group in the past, and the chief factor in the exclusion of Negroes has not been racial prejudice but rather the tendency toward nepotism. The tendency toward nepotism excluded everyone but longshoremen's kinsmen. In other words, it was not directed at blacks but at anyone who was not a member of the longshore group. The most important factor in the resistance to integration more recently has been the desire to protect their traditional recruitment procedures.

The forms of joking behavior reported in other industrial contexts neither resemble the longshore form, except in the vaguest manner, nor fit the original definition of joking behavior given by Radcliffe-Brown. Some form of "joking behavior" may be a common attribute of most social groups, but the extremely rough form of longshore joking behavior may be unique to longshoremen and a few other groups of roughneck workers such as loggers and construction workers. Certainly there is no mention of such behavior for either blue- or white-collar workers in the literature.

The most important of the longshoremens' values is the deeply felt need to manage their leisure time. And this ties them ever more tightly to the union and union affairs, for it is only the union that shelters them from the demands of the employers. This desire to tailor their work and leisure time to fit their personal requirements is not a feature of the longshore group that only came into being with the establishment of the union. It has been a factor on the waterfront since before 1922. The foremost aim of the waterfront employers in 1922 was to establish a "dependable" work force, and this goal, in the sense of maintaining a work force that would always show up for work on demand, was never fully realized. Even the "star men" occasionally failed to show up for work, and the employers were often forced to fall back on casual labor to fill the need for longshoremen. If this one feature of longshore life were removed, the rest of the way of life would soon disappear. It is this management of potential leisure time, combined with the right to "talk back," that the longshoremen refer to when they speak of "freedom and independence." Without this one essential feature, the longshoremen could no longer successfully manage their extra-work economic activities, and there would no longer be as great an incentive to engage in union affairs. Again, the avocations which require the ability to leave the job for extended periods of time would no longer be possible, and the role of the father as an almost omnipresent member of the nuclear family unit would be destroyed with possible detrimental consequences for the entire family structure. It is extremely doubtful that the present longshoremen could adjust to such a change in their way of life without extreme dislocations, and it is certain that any collective bargaining trend that appeared likely to deprive them of this one most salient feature of waterfront employment would lead to a strike.

The absolute necessity of balancing one's work and leisure time in a useful and productive manner is one of the most salient features of pre-industrial life. This feature has been preserved in the Portland longshore group because of the nature of the occupation and the union. In this respect, as in many ways, the Portland longshoremen may be said to represent an old, pre-factory, predominantly native American substratum with a set of values and attitudes very much like those of the Anglo-Saxon elite of skilled workers that dominated the working-class hierarchy of the nineteenth century. This is not to say that they are not a completely modern, urbanized group in every other respect, but only that the set of values and attitudes detailed above, and some of their consequences, are related to and derive from the historical antecedents of the longshore group.

THE FUTURE

Clearly, the way of life of the longshoremen is highly dependent on continuing in waterfront employment and on preserving those conditions of employment obtained and maintained for them by the ILWU. The longshoremen's union and its particular structure and ideology are absolutely essential to the maintenance of the longshore group. It has only been through the bargaining power of the union that job security has been obtained for the longshoremen, and this security is the essential minimum requirement to give meaning to the other conditions of waterfront employment necessary to the continuance of the longshoremen's way of life. It is union control of the hiring hall and the union's jealous protection of the longshoremen's right to work when, where, and for whom they please that completes the set of conditions that are essential to fulfilling the longshoremen's felt need to manage their work and leisure time to fit their personal requirements. These have always been the points upon which the union has differed most with the employers. The issue of maintaining exactly the same set of recruitment and hiring procedures that have been traditional in Portland has also been at the basis of much friction between the Local and the International Unions. This was expressed clearly in the 1966 caucus when the delegates of Local 8 refused to allow any experimentation with the Portland hiring system, and misunderstandings and friction over the traditional recruitment procedure of the Portland Local has caused many of the problems in the process of integrating Negroes into the Portland work force.

It is the union and its peculiarly democratic nature, then, that is responsible for the maintenance of the essential features of the longshore subculture. So long as the union continues to protect the basic job security of the longshoremen and controls the hiring system in the manner that it has in the past, there would seem to be no reason that the Portland longshoremen cannot continue their way of life indefinitely; however, there are three major sources from which the union may expect difficulties. By far the most serious and immediate of these threats is the law. The passage of the Taft-Hartley Act forced the union to adopt the complicated measures incorporated in the Pedro Formula in order to comply with provisions of the act forbidding the preferential hiring of union members. And the "Bill of Rights" section of the Labor-Management Reporting and Disclosure Act of 1959, which was intended to protect the rights of union members, has disrupted the order of union meetings by requiring a secret ballot vote on trivial assessments when the traditional democratic procedure had always been a hand or voice vote. In the past this Act has also prevented certain union members from holding office. The greatest threat from the law, however, stems from Section 14 (b) of the National Labor Relations Act. This insertion from the Taft-Hartley Act allows states to prohibit the union shop by means of "right to work" laws. Clearly, a waterfront union could not hope to operate without the preferential hiring of union members, because the employers need only avoid hiring the union men to destroy the union entirely.

Automation poses not only a threat to the longshoremen's way of life, but a threat to his very livelihood, and indeed a threat to the entire economic structure of the modern world. That the machine may replace the stevedore in the not too distant future is well known to all of the longshoremen and their union officials. The history of the Portland waterfront is a history of constantly increasing mechanization. More machines have been introduced into longshore work almost every year, but the longshoremen have never suffered from this incursion; rather, the machine has made life easier for them by removing much of the backbreaking

One of the new automated ships. Vans of cargo are simply rolled on and off by large lift trucks. (Photo by Gordon Clark)

labor that was for so long a feature of longshore work. While the introduction of simple labor saving devices, such as winches and lift trucks, has had a significant impact on the size of the longshore work force, it is quite different from the introduction of completely automated systems that would allow a cargo ship to be discharged and loaded without the services of a single longshoreman, and such systems are being drafted at present.

The longshoremen's union is not unaware of this problem and has taken steps to meet the problem before it arises. The ILWU initiated negotiations on a mechanization and modernization program in 1957 that was culminated in the 1960 Mechanization and Modernization Agreement between the International Longshoremen's and Warehousemen's Union and the Pacific Maritime Association. This contract secured partial guarantees of security for the longshoremen, a large increase in wages, increased pensions and benefits for the older men, a vested interest of $7,920 for longshoremen when they retired, and the retirement age was reduced to sixty-two. In return, the union gave the PMA sweeping powers to introduce labor saving devices and relaxed or removed most of the restrictive union rules dealing with manning scales. Moreover, the union agreed to *assist* the PMA in their attempts to mechanize the longshore industry. This contract has worked so well that both union and management have profited significantly from its operation, and a new mechanization agreement was concluded between the ILWU and

PMA in 1966 which doubled the previous pensions and increased the vested interest of the retiring longshoremen to $13,000 per man. And again the PMA was given the power to introduce more labor saving devices and methods (Hagel and Goldblatt 1963).

This sort of approach to the problem of mechanization represents a great departure from the previous union practice of resisting the introduction of labor saving devices and methods which has made mechanization expensive for employers and has at times put unions completely out of business. Nonetheless, even this new approach is only a temporary expedient, because further mechanization is certain to reduce the union membership to the point that they have no further economic bargaining power. A local union with 1200 members is one thing and a local union with only 100 members is quite another, and this is the predictable outcome of increasing automation.

However, another factor has entered the picture with this increase in mechanization. More and more heavy equipment is being introduced on the waterfront, and longshoremen are being trained to operate this equipment. The increasing size and complexity of the machines which longshoremen operate require more and more in the way of highly specialized skills and training. There is a quantum difference between a two ton steam cargo winch and a thirty ton high speed ore unloader. The present trend is for the Portland longshoremen, and all other longshoremen on the Pacific Coast, to become specialized heavy equipment operators. The job is becoming ever more technical in nature and the predictable outcome of this trend is that all of the longshoremen will one day be heavy equipment operators of this order. Such highly trained men are harder and much more expensive to replace, and it is possible that the longshoremen's future position will be much strengthened by this trend. If so, they may be able to maintain their way of life for some indefinite period, but their numbers are sure to be severely depleted.

Internal dissension and the centrifugal force of individualism have always threatened the longshore group by threatening the viability of the local union; however, the history of conflict on the Portland waterfront has made most of the longshoremen aware of the necessity, if not the desirability, of continued cooperation and collective action. It is only the very responsive nature of the union that has allowed the conditions to exist under which the extremely individualistic longshoremen have been willing to surrender a portion of their freedom for the good of the organization. This is an example of enlightened self-interest. The longshoremen will not continue to surrender their freedom of action and individualism under any and all circumstances simply for the purpose of preserving an organization: they are pragmatists and not idealists. The union has "delivered the goods"; therefore, the union should be protected and supported.

CONCLUSIONS

The Portland longshoremen form an internal urban community bearing a somewhat distinctive subculture similar to that of many other roughneck workers such as lumberjacks, miners, oilfield and construction workers and the like. The community is bound together by tradition, kinship, and a series of community institutions centering around the longshoremen's union. The community cannot be defined in territorial terms unless we wish to include all of the other residents of the greater Portland area and a certain number of citizens of the state of Washington. It can only be defined in social terms, in terms of being a cohesive social group, with distinctive community institutions, and an internally derived identity.

It is also clear that such an occupationally based community cannot be regarded as an entity completely or even partially isolated from the city, the state, or the nation, for by the very fact of their occupation they are tightly tied to the fabric of the economic system of the nation and indeed of the world; it is the very fact of international trade that supplies them with cargo to load into the holds of ships from many nations. Nonetheless, they are a discrete entity within the framework of the larger society, bound to one another in tight role networks that do not encompass the other residents of the Portland area or even the other people with whom they work such as sailors, truck drivers, clerks, and office personnel.

No claim is advanced here that all or even many occupations represent dispersed urban communities. This is a purely empirical question as is the question as to whether other dispersed communities of any kind exist within urban centers or urban societies, although the San Francisco and Seattle longshoremen seem to present a similar picture and Lipset's work indicates that at least many typographers form just such dispersed occupationally based urban communities (1962).

As anthropologists move from studies of rural migrants to the city and other groups that are not integrated into the structure of urban society, that are still in the process of adjusting to the urban milieu, we must be prepared to abandon the territorial concept of community where it is no longer useful. And eventually, we will have to take this step, for we cannot truly and fully understand the problems of migrants and their adjustment to the city unless we understand the nature of the subcultures and communities of the people to whom the migrants must adjust. It is much overlooked that as people become integrated into the structure of the city, they adjust to and take up the attitudes and way of life of older urban residents. Thus, the nature of such urban groups are as important to the adjustment of migrants to the city as are the natures and situations of migrant or slum communities. It is also the case that all internal urban groups, normal in the sense that they are well integrated into the structure of the city and society, must constantly be adjusting to the rapid social and industrial change that has characterized all industrial societies, and that they would seem to have mechanisms for doing so in a relatively efficient manner. It might seem that studies of such groups would be enlightening in terms of the adjustments of newcomers to the city.

I am not advocating abandonment of the territorial concept of community, but rather that the distinction between territorial aggregates and social groups should be clearly made in urban anthropology, and that it may often be the case in the urban situation that the social group based on grounds other than contiguous residence may be a more fruitful unit of analysis than the territorial unit.

Glossary

Cargo inspector: A longshoreman who is notorious for pilfering cargo.

Caulk boots: Pronounced "cork boots." Work boots with spikes set in the soles to give traction when working on slippery logs.

Checker: A ship's clerk. A man who keeps tally on cargo being moved over the docks or on or off the ships.

Chippy: A person who seeks illicit sex. In some dialects only a woman, but applied by the longshoremen to both men and women.

Chisel: To cut short the amount of recorded work time for which a longshoreman is paid.

Coaming: The raised edge around the hatch.

Fink: A strikebreaker or informer. An extremely insulting term.

Gang: The longshore shipboard work team: a foreman, two or three winch operators, two sling men and four to eight hold men.

Goon: A muscle man; a strong-arm man.

Hatch: The opening into a cargo hold.

Hold: The cargo space in a ship.

Hold man: A longshoreman who works in the ship's hold.

Hook (or lumberhook): A tool used by longshoremen for pulling on large boards or heavy boxes. Similar to a hay hook.

Logger: A lumberjack. The term "lumberjack" is almost never used in the Pacific Northwest among loggers or related workers.

Longshoreman: A worker who loads and unloads ships. Synonymous with stevedore. Originally alongshoreman.

Pie card: A union official with life tenure in office.

Sabotage: A work slowdown. Anything that disrupts the pace of the work.

Scab: A strikebreaker.

Shape up: A system of hiring where the longshoremen come to a dock and form a circle of men. The hiring boss stands in the middle and picks the men he wants to work that day.

Sling man: The longshoreman who hooks up or unhooks loads for the ship's hoisting gear.

Star gang: A preferred gang: a gang that is considered superior by its employer.

Stevedore: A longshoreman.

Stevedore company: A firm that contracts to load and unload ships.

Walking boss: A foreman who supervises several gangs.

Winch: A machine used to hoist cargo onto or off a ship. A winch resembles a gigantic fishing reel operated by a large reversible motor so that it can take in or pay out the steel cables used in hoisting.

Wobbly: A member of the Industrial Workers of the World, the I.W.W.

References

Anastasio, Angelo, 1960, "Port Haven, a Changing Northwestern Community." Pullman: *Washington(State) Agricultural Experiment Station Bulletin 616.*

Banton, Michael, 1957, *West African City.* London: Oxford University Press.

Barnes, Charles B., 1915, *The Longshoremen.* Philadelphia: Survey Associates, Inc.

Bell, Daniel, 1956, *Work and Its Discontents.* Boston: Beacon Press.

————, 1959, "The Racket-ridden Longshoremen," *Dissent,* VI, Autumn, pp. 417–29.

Bjork, Kenneth O., 1958, *West of the Great Divide: Norwegian Migration to the Pacific Coast, 1847–1893.* Northfield, Minn.: Norwegian–American Historical Association.

Blowner, Robert, 1964, *Alienation and Freedom: The Factory Worker and His Industry.* Chicago: University of Chicago Press.

Buchanan, Roger B., 1964, "History of the 1934 Waterfront Strike in Portland, Oregon." Unpublished Master's Thesis. Eugene: University of Oregon.

Buechley, R. W., R. M. Drake, and Lester Breslow, 1958, "Height, Weight, and Mortality in a Population of Longshoremen." *Journal of Chronic Diseases* Vol. 7, No. 5, pp. 363–378.

Burleson, Noel D., 1964, "Proletarian Perspectives, an Anthropology of Industry." Ph.D. Thesis. Cambridge: Harvard University.

Cox, Archibald and Derek C. Bok, 1962, *Statutory Supplement to Cases on Labor Law.* Brooklyn, N.Y.: The Foundation Press.

————, 1965, *Cases and Materials on Labor Law.* Brooklyn, N.Y.: The Foundation Press.

Dyer, William G., 1964, "Family Reactions to the Father's Job." In *Blue Collar World,* Shostak and Gomberg, eds., Englewood Cliffs, N.J.: Prentice-Hall.

Eggan, F. and Max Gluckman, 1965, "Introduction." In *The Relevance of Models for Social Anthropology,* M. Banton, ed., London: Tavistock Pub.

Epstein, A. L., 1961, "The Network and Social Organization." *Rhodes-Livingston Journal,* 29:29–62.

Foner, Philip, 1965, "The Industrial Workers of the World." *History of the Labor Movement in the United States,* IV. New York: International Publishers.

Glazer, Nathan and Patrick Moynihan, 1963, *Beyond the Melting Pot.* Cambridge: The M. I. T. Press.

Gordon, Milton M., 1958, *Social Class in American Sociology.* New York: McGraw-Hill.

Gordon, Milton M. and Charles H. Anderson, 1964, "The Blue-collar Worker at Leisure." In *Blue Collar World,* Shostak and Gomberg, eds., Englewood Cliffs, N.J.: Prentice-Hall.

Gouldner, Alvin W., 1954, *Patterns of Industrial Bureaucracy.* New York: The Free Press.

————, 1954, *Wildcat Strike*. Yellow Springs, Ohio: Antioch Press.

Hagel, Otto and Louis Goldblatt, 1963, *Men and Machines*. San Francisco: International Longshoremen's and Warehousemen's Union and the Pacific Maritime Association.

Hamilton, Richard F., 1964, "The Behavior and Values of Skilled Workers." In *Blue Collar World*, Shostak and Gomberg, eds., Englewood Cliffs, N.J.: Prentice-Hall.

Hatt, P. K., 1972, "Occupation and Social Stratification." *American Journal of Sociology*, LV, No. 6.

Hughes, Everett C., 1958, *Men and Their Work*. New York: The Free Press.

Hurvitz, Everett C., 1964, "Marital Strain in the Blue-collar Family." In *Blue Collar World*, Shostak and Gomberg, eds., Englewood Cliffs, N.J.: Prentice-Hall.

International Longshoremen's and Warehousemen's Union, 1952, *Pedro Formula*. San Francisco: ILWU.

————, 1960, *Constitution and Bylaws*. Portland: ILWU Local 8.

————, 1966, Summarized Minutes: Longshore, Clerks, and Walking Boss Caucus. July 13-14, p. 10.

————, 1966, *The Dispatcher*. San Francisco: ILWU.

————, 1966, *The Hook*. Portland: ILWU Local 8.

————, 1966, Minutes of the Membership Meetings. Portland: ILWU Local 8.

ILWU and the Pacific Maritime Association, 1966, Pacific Coast Longshore Contract Document.

Kornbluh, Joyce L., ed., 1964, *Rebel Voices: An I. W. W. Anthology*. Ann Arbor: University of Michigan Press.

Larrowe, Charles P., 1955, *Shape-up and Hiring Hall*. Berkeley: University of California Press.

————, 1955, *Maritime Labor Relations on the Great Lakes*. Michigan State University Labor and Industrial Relations Center.

Lascelles, E. C. and S. S. Bullock, 1924, "Dock Labour and Decasualization." *Studies in Economics and Political Sciences*, No. 75, London: London School of Economics and Political Science.

LePlay, F., 1879, *Les Ouvriers Européens*. Paris: Alfred Mame et fils.

Lewis, Oscar, 1950, "An Anthropological Approach to Family Studies." *American Journal of Sociology*, LV, No. 5.

————, 1952, "Urbanization without Breakdown: A Case Study." *Scientific Monthly*, July, pp. 31–41.

————, 1965, *La Vida*. New York: Random House.

Lipset, S. M., Martin Trow, and James Coleman, 1962, *Union Democracy: the Internal Politics of the Typographical Union*. Garden City, N.Y.: Anchor Books, Doubleday.

Little, Kenneth, 1965, *West African Urbanization: A Study of Voluntary Associations in Social Change*. Cambridge: Cambridge University Press.

Mangin, William, 1959, "The Role of Regional Associations in the Adaptation of the Rural Population in Peru." *Sociologus*, 9, pp. 23–25.

Mayer, Kurt B. and Sidney Goldstein, 1964, "Manual Workers as Small Businessmen." In *Blue Collar World*, Shostak and Gomberg, eds., Englewood Cliffs, N.J.: Prentice-Hall.

Miller, S. M. and Frank Riessman, 1964, "The Working Class Subculture: A New View." In *Blue Collar World*, Shostak and Gomberg, eds., Englewood Cliffs, N.J.: Prentice-Hall.

Perlman, Selig, 1966, *A Theory of the Labor Movement*. New York: Augustus M. Kelley.

Philpott, Stuart B., n.d., "The Union Hiring Hall as a Labour Market: A Socio-logical Analysis." *British Journal of Industrial Relations*, III, pp. 17–30.

Pollard, Lancaster, 1951, "The Pacific Northwest: a Regional Study." *Oregon Historical Society Quarterly*, Portland: Oregon Historical Society.

Portland Stevedore Company, 1923, Correspondence, ILWU Library.

Radcliffe–Brown, A. R., 1952, *Structure and Function in Primitive Society*. New York: The Free Press.

Record, Jane C., 1967, "Race, Jobs, and Unions." Unpublished mimeographed report. Northwest Scientific Association Meetings, April.

Redfield, Robert, 1955, *The Little Community: Viewpoints for the Study of a Human Whole*. Chicago: University of Chicago Press.

Renshaw, Patrick, 1967, *The Wobblies*. Garden City, N.Y.: Doubleday.

Rodman, Hyman, 1964, "Middle-class Misconceptions about Lower-class Families." In *Blue Collar World*, Shostak and Gomberg, eds., Englewood Cliffs, N.J.: Prentice-Hall.

Roethlisberger, F. J. and William J. Dickson, 1937, *Management and the Worker*. Cambridge: Harvard University Press.

Seidman, J., Jack London, and Bernard Karsh, 1951, "Leadership in a Local Union." *American Journal of Sociology*, LVI, No. 3.

Shostak, Arthur B. and William Gomberg, 1964, *Blue Collar World: Studies of the American Worker*. Englewood Cliffs, N.J.: Prentice-Hall.

Sinclair, Upton, 1905, *The Jungle*. New York: New American Library.

Southall, A. W., 1959, "An Operational Theory of Role." *Human Relations*, 12: 17–34.

———, 1961, *Social Change in Modern Africa*. London: Oxford University Press.

Steward, J. H., 1956, *The People of Puerto Rico*. Urbana, Ill.: University of Illinois Press.

Swados, Harvey, 1957, *On the Line*. Boston: Little, Brown.

———, 1961, "West-coast Waterfront—the End of an Era." *Dissent*, Autumn.

Tomlinson, Lawrence E., 1944, "Factors Influencing the Immigration of the Foreign Born to the U.S. and to Oregon." Unpublished mimeograph.

"Union Labor: Less Militant, More Affluent," 1965. *Time*, September 17, pp. 42–43.

Warner, W. Lloyd and J. O. Low, 1947, *The Social System of the Modern Factory*. New Haven: Yale University Press.

Warner, W. Lloyd, 1953, *American Life*. Chicago: University of Chicago Press.

Waterfront Employers' Union, 1919, Correspondence, ILWU Library.

Whyte, William Foote, 1943, *Street Corner Society*. Chicago: University of Chicago Press.

Recommended readings

Gouldner, Alvin W., 1954, *Patterns of Industrial Bureaucracy*. New York: The Free Press.
   A fine description of the relations between mine and factory workers and their employers. An excellent treatise on the values of the workers and the interaction between these values and bureaucratic goals.
Hagel, Otto, and Louis Goldblatt, 1965, *Men and Machines*. San Francisco: International Longshoremen's and Warehousemen's Union and the Pacific Maritime Association.
   A good description of the Mechanization and Modernization agreement and its effect on the longshore industry. Many excellent pictures of longshoremen working.
Hughes, Everett C., 1958, *Men and Their Work*. New York: The Free Press.
   An incisive examination of the effects of occupation on professionals. Much overlooked but very good.
Kesey, Ken, 1964, *Sometimes a Great Notion*. New York: Viking.
   This novel about Oregon loggers is perhaps the best source available for gaining a very personal sort of insight into the values and life style of Northwestern roughneck workers. It is also an excellent novel.
Kornbluh, Joyce L., ed., 1964, *Rebel Voices: An I.W.W. Anthology*. Ann Arbor: University of Michigan Press.
   A fine collection of Wobbly literature, chronologically arranged, with introductory essays and explanations by Kornbluh. This book also contains most of the more popular I.W.W. songs.
Larrowe, Charles P., 1955, *Shape-up and Hiring Hall*. Berkeley: University of California Press.
   A comparison of the history, nature, and functions of the longshore hiring systems in New York and Seattle. A good starting place for research.
Lipset, S. M., Martin Trow, and James Coleman, 1962. *Union Democracy: the Internal Politics of the Typographical Union*. Garden City, N.Y.: Anchor Books, Doubleday.
   A description of the political process in a trade union.
Mayo, Elton, 1960, *The Human Problems of an Industrial Civilization*. New York: Viking.
   The classic definition of the human problems that arise in industry. First published in 1929, but still applicable.
Quin, Mike, 1949, *The Big Strike*. Olema, Calif.: Olema Publishing Company.
   A union account of the 1934 strike in San Francisco. Revealing of the way the longshoremen felt about this strike.
Russel, Maud, 1966, *Men along the Shore*. New York: Brussel and Brussel.
   A very bad book which is included here only to warn students against taking

it seriously. A romanticized apology for the notoriously corrupt administration of Joe Ryan. More than biased, but perhaps worth looking at to see how badly a naive researcher can be hoodwinked.

Shostak, Arthur B., and William Gomberg, 1964, *Blue Collar World: Studies of the American Worker*. Englewood Cliffs, N.J.: Prentice-Hall.

A collection of sociological articles dealing with blue-collar workers. The articles by S. M. Miller and Frank Riessman are outstanding statements of the theoretical problems of this field of study. Many other excellent articles.